Solitude

Part I

by

Johann Georg Zimmermann

Solitude
Part I
by Johann Georg Zimmermann

ISBN: 978-93-69072-21-7

Published by

DOUBLE 9 BOOKS

2/13-B, Ansari Road
Daryaganj, New Delhi – 110002
info@double9books.com
www.double9books.com
Tel. 011-40042856

ABOUT THE AUTHOR

Johann Georg Ritter von Zimmermann was a Swiss philosopher, naturalist, and physician, born on December 8, 1728, in Brugg, Switzerland. Zimmermann is known for his philosophical writings, particularly his exploration of solitude in the late 18th century. He served as the private physician to both George III of Britain and Frederick the Great of Prussia, an influential role that positioned him in the courts of Europe. Zimmermann's works blended naturalism, philosophy, and the human experience, offering insights into the nature of human emotions and intellectual growth. His writings, including Solitude, emphasized the importance of introspection and self-reflection for personal well-being and creativity. Throughout his life, Zimmermann engaged deeply with the intellectual currents of his time, contributing significantly to discussions on mental health and human nature. He died on October 7, 1795, in Hanover, Germany, at the age of 66. Zimmermann's legacy endures through his thought-provoking works that continue to be valued for their exploration of solitude, human nature, and the mind. He had one child, Katharina von Zimmermann, and remains an important figure in the history of European philosophy and medicine.

CONTENTS

PREFACE

Weak and delicate minds may, perhaps, be alarmed by the title of this work. The word *solitude*, may possibly engender melancholy ideas; but they have only to read a few pages to be undeceived. The author is not one of those extravagant misanthropists who expect that men, formed by nature for the enjoyments of society, and impelled continually towards it by a multitude of powerful and invincible propensities, should seek refuge in forests, and inhabit the dreary cave or lonely cell; he is a friend to the species, a rational philosopher, and the virtuous citizen, who, encouraged by the esteem of his sovereign, endeavors to enlighten the minds of his fellow creatures upon a subject of infinite importance to them, the attainment of true felicity.

No writer appears more completely convinced than M. Zimmerman, that man is born for society, or feels its duties with more refined sensibility.

It is the nature of human society, and its correspondent duties, which he here undertakes to examine. The important characters of father, husband, son, and citizen, impose on man a variety of obligations, which are always dear to virtuous minds, and establish between him, his country, his family, and his friends, relations too necessary and attractive to be disregarded.

> "What wonder, therefore, since th' endearing ties
>
> Of passion link the universal kind
>
> Of man so close; what wonder if to search
>
> This common nature through the various change
>
> Of sex, of age, and fortune, and the frame
>
> Of each peculiar, draw the busy mind
>
> With unresisted charms? The spacious west,
>
> And all the teeming regions of the south,
>
> Hold not a quarry to the curious flight,
>
> Of knowledge half so tempting or so fair,
>
> As man to man."

But it is not amidst tumultuous joys and noisy pleasures; in the chimeras of ambition, or the illusions of self-love; in the indulgence of feeling, or the gratification of desire, that men must expect to feel the charms of those mutual ties which link them so firmly to society. It is not in such enjoyments that men can feel the dignity of those duties, the performance of which nature has rendered productive of so many pleasures, or hope to taste that true felicity which results from an independent mind and a contented heart: a felicity seldom sought after, only because it is so little known, but which every individual may find within his own bosom. Who, alas! does not constantly experience the necessity of entering into that sacred asylum to search for consolation under the real or imaginary misfortunes of life, or to alleviate indeed more frequently the fatigue of its painful pleasures? Yes, all men, from the mercenary trader, who sinks under the anxiety of his daily task, to the proud statesman, intoxicated by the incense of popular applause, experience the desire of terminating their arduous career. Every bosom feels an anxiety for repose, and fondly wishes to steal from the vortex of a busy and perturbed life, to enjoy the tranquillity of solitude.

> "Hackney'd in business, wearied at that oar
>
> Which thousands, once chain'd fast to, quit no more,
>
> But which, when life at ebb, runs weak and low,
>
> All wish, or seem to wish, they could forego;
>
> The statesman, lawyer, merchant, man of trade,
>
> Pant for the refuge of a peaceful shade
>
> Where all his long anxieties forgot,
>
> Amidst the charms of a sequester'd spot,
>
> Or recollected only to gild o'er
>
> And add a smile to what was sweet before,
>
> He may possess the joys he thinks he sees,
>
> Lay his old age upon the lap of ease,
>
> Improve the remnant of his wasted span,
>
> And having liv'd a trifler, die a man."

It is under the peaceful shades of solitude that the mind regenerates and acquires fresh force; it is there alone that the happy can enjoy the fulness of felicity, or the miserable forget their wo; it is there that the bosom of sensibility experiences its most delicious emotions; it is there that creative genius frees itself from the thraldom of society, and surrenders itself to the impetuous rays of an ardent imagination. To this desired goal all our ideas and desires perpetually tend. "There is," says Dr. Johnson, "scarcely any writer, who has not celebrated the happiness of rural privacy, and delighted himself and his readers with the melody of birds, the whisper of groves, and the murmurs of rivulets; nor any man eminent for extent of capacity, or greatness of exploits, that has not left behind him some memorials of lonely wisdom and silent dignity."

The original work from which the following pages are selected, consists of four large volumes, which have acquired the universal approbation of the German empire, and obtained the suffrages of an empress celebrated for the superior brilliancy of her mind, and who has signified her approbation in the most flattering manner.

On the 26th of January, 1785, a courier, dispatched by the Russian envoy at Hamburg, presented M. Zimmerman with a small casket, in the name of her majesty the empress of Russia. The casket contained a ring set round with diamonds of an extraordinary size and lustre; and a gold medal bearing on one side the portrait of the empress, and on the other the date of the happy reformation of the Russian empire. This present the empress accompanied with a letter, written with her own hand, containing these remarkable words:—"To M. Zimmerman, counsellor of state, and physician to his Britannic majesty, to thank him for the excellent precepts he has given to mankind in his treatise upon solitude."

LIFE OF ZIMMERMAN

John George Zimmerman was born on the 8th day of December, 1728, at Brugg, a small town in the canton of Berne.

His father, John Zimmerman, was eminently distinguished as an able and eloquent member of the provincial council. His mother, who was equally respected and beloved for her good sense, easy manners, and modest virtues, was the daughter of the celebrated Pache, whose extraordinary learning and great abilities, had contributed to advance him to a seat in the parliament of Paris.

The father of Zimmerman undertook the arduous task of superintending his education, and, by the assistance of able preceptors, instructed him in the rudiments of all the useful and ornamental sciences, until he had attained the age of fourteen years, when he sent him to the university of Berne, where, under Kirchberger, the historian and professor of rhetoric, and Altman, the celebrated Greek professor, he studied, for three years, philology and the belles lettres, with unremitting assiduity and attention.

Having passed nearly five years at the university, he began to think of applying the stores of information he had acquired to the purposes of active life; and after mentioning the subject cursorily to a few relations, he immediately resolved to follow the practice of physic. The extraordinary fame of Haller, who had recently been promoted by king George II. to a professorship in the university of Gottingen, resounded at this time throughout Europe: and Zimmerman determined to prosecute his studies in physic under the auspices of this great and celebrated master. He was admitted into the university on the 12th of September, 1747, and obtained his degree on the 14th of August, 1751. To relax his mind from severer studies, he cultivated a complete knowledge of the English language, and became so great a proficient in the polite and elegant literature of this country, that the British poets, particularly Shakspeare, Pope, and Thomson, were as familiar to him as his favorite authors, Homer and Virgil. Every moment, in short, of the four years he passed at Gottingen, was employed in the improvement of his mind; and so early as the year 1751, he produced a work in which he discovered the dawnings of that extraordinary genius which afterwards spread abroad with so much effulgence. [1]

During the early part of his residence at Berne, he published many excellent essays on various subjects in the Helvetic Journal; particularly a work on the talents and erudition of Haller. This grateful tribute, to the just merits of his friend and benefactor, he afterwards enlarged into a complete history of his life and writings, as a scholar, a philosopher, a physician, and a man.

The health of Haller, which had suffered greatly by the severity of study, seemed to decline in proportion as his fame increased; and, obtaining permission to leave Gottingen, he repaired to Berne, to try, by the advice and assistance of Zimmerman, to restore, if possible, his decayed constitution. The benefits he experienced in a short time were so great, that he determined to relinquish his professorship, and to pass the remainder of his days in that city. In the family of Haller, lived a young lady, nearly related to him, whose maiden name was Mely, and whose husband, M. Stek, had been sometime dead. Zimmerman became deeply enamored of her charms: he offered her his hand in marriage; and they were united at the altar in the bands of mutual affection.

Soon after his union with this amiable woman, the situation of physician to the town of Brugg became vacant, which he was invited by the inhabitants to fill; and he accordingly relinquished the pleasures and advantages he enjoyed at Berne and returned to the place of his nativity, with a view to settle himself there for life. His time, however, was not so entirely engrossed by the duties of his profession, as to prevent him from indulging his mind in the pursuits of literature; and he read almost every work of reputed merit, whether of physic, or moral philosophy, belles lettres, history, voyages, or even novels and romances, which the various presses of Europe from time to time produced. The novels and romances of England, in particular, gave him great delight.

But the amusements which Brugg afforded were extremely confined: and he fell into a state of nervous langor, or rather into a peevish dejection of spirits, neglecting society, and devoting himself almost entirely to a retired and sedentary life.

Under these circumstances, this excellent and able man passed fourteen years of an uneasy life; but neither his increasing practice, the success of his literary pursuits, [2] the exhortations of his friends, nor the endeavors of his family, were able to remove the melancholy and discontent that preyed continually on his mind. After some fruitless efforts to please him, he was in the beginning of April, 1768, appointed by the interest of Dr. Tissot, and baron Hockstettin, to the post of principal physician to the king of Great Britain, at Hanover; and he departed from Brugg, to take possession of his new office, on the 4th of July, in the same year. Here he was plunged into the deepest affliction by the loss of his amiable wife, who after many years of lingering sufferance, and pious resignation, expired in his arms, on the 23d of June, 1770; an event which he has described in the following work, with eloquent tenderness and sensibility. His children too, were to him additional causes of the keenest anguish and the deepest distress. His daughter had from her earliest infancy, discovered symptoms of consumption, so strong and inveterate as to defy all the powers of medicine, and which, in the summer of 1781, destroyed her life. The character of this amiable girl, and the feelings of her afflicted father on this melancholy event, his own pen has very affectingly described in the following work.

But the state and condition of his son was still more distressing to his feelings than even the death of his beloved daughter. This unhappy youth, who, while he was at the university, discovered the finest fancy and the soundest understanding, either from a malignant and inveterate species of scrofula, with which he had been periodically tortured from his earliest infancy, or from too close an application to study, fell very early in life into a state of bodily infirmity and mental langor, which terminated in the month of December, 1777, in a total derangement of his faculties; and he has now continued, in spite of every endeavor to restore him, a perfect idiot for more than twenty years.

The domestic comforts of Zimmerman were now almost entirely destroyed; till at length, he fixed upon the daughter of M. Berger, the king's physician at Lunenbourg, and niece to baron de Berger, as a person in every respect qualified to make him happy, and they were united to each other in marriage about the beginning of October, 1782. Zimmerman was nearly thirty years older than his bride: but genius and good sense are always young: and the similarity of their characters obliterated all recollection of disparity of age.

It was at this period that he composed his great and favorite work on solitude, thirty years after the publication of his first essay on the subject. It consists of four volumes in quarto: the two first of which were published in 1784; and the remaining volumes in 1786. "A work," says Tissot, "which will always be read with as much profit as pleasure, as it contains the most sublime conceptions, the greatest sagacity of observation, and extreme propriety of application, much ability in the choice of examples, and (what I cannot commend too highly, because I can say nothing that does him so much honor, nor give him any praise that would be more gratifying to his own heart) a constant anxiety for the interest of religion, with the sacred and solemn truths of which his mind was most devoutly impressed."

The king of Prussia, while he was reviewing his troops in Silesia, in the autumn of the year 1785, caught a severe cold, which settled on his lungs and in the course of nine months brought on symptoms of an approaching dropsy. Zimmerman, by two very flattering letters of the 6th and 16th of June, 1786, was solicited by his majesty to attend him, and he arrived at Potzdam on the 23d of the same month; but he immediately discovered that his royal patient had but little hopes of recovery; and, after trying the effect of such medicines as he thought most likely to afford relief, he returned to Hanover on the 11th of July following. [3] But it was not Frederick alone who discovered his abilities. When in the year 1788, the melancholy state of the king of England's health alarmed the affection of his subjects, and produced an anxiety throughout Europe for his recovery, the government of Hanover dispatched Zimmerman to Holland, that he might be nearer London, in case his presence there became necessary; and he continued at the Hague until all danger was over.

Zimmerman was the first who had the courage to unveil the dangerous principles of the new philosophers, and to exhibit to the eyes of the German princes the risk they ran in neglecting to oppose the progress of so formidable a league. He convinced many of them, and particularly the emperor Leopold II. that the views of these *illuminated* conspirators were the destruction of Christianity, and the subversion of all regular government. These exertions, while they contributed to lessen the danger which threatened his adopted country, greatly impaired his health.

In the month of November, 1794, he was obliged to have recourse to strong opiates to procure even a short repose: his appetite decreased; his strength failed him; and he became so weak and emaciated, that, in January 1795, he was induced to visit a few particular patients in his carriage, it was painful to him to write a prescription, and he frequently fainted while ascending to the room. These symptoms were followed by a dizziness in his head, which obliged him to relinquish all business. At length the axis of his brain gave way, and reduced him to such a state of mental imbecility, that he was haunted continually by an idea that the enemy was plundering his house, and that he and his family were reduced to a state of misery and want. His medical friends, particularly Dr. Wichman, by whom he was constantly attended, contributed their advice and assistance to restore him to health; and conceiving that a journey and a change of air were the best remedies that could be applied, they sent him to Eutin, in the duchy of Holstein, where he continued three months, and about the month of June, 1795, returned to Hanover greatly recovered. But the fatal dart had infixed itself too deeply to be entirely removed; he soon afterwards relapsed into his former imbecility, and barely existed in lingering sufferance for many months, refusing to take any medicines, and scarcely any food; continually harassed and distressed by the cruel allusion of poverty, which again haunted his imagination. At certain intervals his mind seemed to recover only for the purpose of rendering him sensible of his approaching dissolution; for he frequently said to his physicians, "My death I perceive will be slow and painful;" and, about fourteen hours before he died, he exclaimed, "Leave me to myself; I am dying." At length his emaciated body and exhausted mind sunk beneath the burden of mortality, and he expired without a groan, on the 7th October, 1795, aged 66 years and ten months.

Chapter I
Introduction

Solitude is that intellectual state in which the mind voluntarily surrenders itself to its own reflections. The philosopher, therefore, who withdraws his attention from every external object to the contemplation of his own ideas, is not less solitary than he who abandons society, and resigns himself entirely to the calm enjoyments of lonely life.

The word "solitude" does not necessarily import a total retreat from the world and its concerns: the dome of domestic society, a rural village, or the library of a learned friend, may respectively become the seat of solitude, as well as the silent shade of some sequestered spot far removed from all connection with mankind.

A person may be frequently solitary without being alone. The haughty baron, proud of his illustrious descent, is solitary unless he is surrounded by his equals: a profound reasoner is solitary at the tables of the witty and the gay. The mind may be as abstracted amidst a numerous assembly; as much withdrawn from every surrounding object; as retired and concentrated in itself; as solitary, in short, as a monk in his cloister, or a hermit in his cave. Solitude, indeed, may exist amidst the tumultuous intercourse of an agitated city as well as in the peaceful shades of rural retirement; at London and at Paris, as well as on the plains of Thebes and the deserts of Nitria.

The mind, when withdrawn from external objects, adopts, freely and extensively, the dictates of its own ideas, and implicitly follows the taste, the temperament, the inclination, and the genius, of its possessor. Sauntering through the cloisters of the Magdalen convent at Hidelshiem, I could not observe, without a smile, an aviary of canary birds, which had been bred in the cell of a female devotee. A gentleman of Brabant, lived five-and-twenty years without ever going out of his house, entertaining himself during that long period with forming a magnificent cabinet of pictures and paintings. Even unfortunate captives, who are doomed to perpetual imprisonment, may soften the rigors of their fate, by resigning themselves, as far as their situation will permit, to the ruling passion of their souls. Michael Ducret, the Swiss philosopher, while he was confined in the castle of Aarburg, in the canton of Berne, in Swisserland, measured the height of the Alps: and while the mind of baron Trenck, during his imprisonment at Magdebourg, was with incessant anxiety, fabricating projects to effect his escape, general Walrave, the companion of his captivity, contentedly passed his time in feeding chickens.

The human mind, in proportion as it is deprived of external resources, sedulously labors to find within itself the means of happiness, learns to rely with confidence on its own exertions, and gains with greater certainty the power of being happy.

A work, therefore, on the subject of solitude, appeared to me likely to facilitate man in his search after true felicity.

Unworthy, however, as the dissipation and pleasures of the world appear to me to be, of the avidity with which they are pursued, I equally disapprove of the extravagant system which inculcates a total dereliction of society; which will be found, when seriously examined, to be equally romantic and impracticable. To be able to live independent of all assistance, except from our own power, is, I acknowledge, a noble effort of the human mind; but it is equally great and dignified to learn the art of enjoying the comforts of society with happiness to ourselves, and with utility to others.

While, therefore, I exhort my readers to listen to the advantages of *occasional retirement*, I warn them against that dangerous excess into which some of the disciples of this philosophy have fallen; an excess equally repugnant to reason and religion. May I happily steer through all the dangers with which my subject is surrounded; sacrifice nothing to prejudice; offer no violation to truth; and gain the approbation of the judicious and reflecting! If affliction shall feel one ray of comfort, or melancholy, released from a portion of its horrors, raise its down cast head; if I shall convince the lover of rural life, that all the finer springs of pleasure dry up and decay in the intense joys of crowded cities, and that the warmest emotions of the heart become there cold and torpid; if I shall evince the superior pleasures of the country; how many resources rural life affords against the langors of indolence; what purity of sentiment, what peaceful repose, what exalted happiness, is inspired by verdant meads, and the view of lively flocks quitting their rich pastures to seek, with the declining sun, their evening folds: how highly the romantic scenery of a wild and striking country, interspersed with cottages, the habitations of a happy, free, contented race of men, elevates the soul; how far more interesting to the heart are the joyful occupations of rural industry, than the dull and tasteless entertainments of a dissipated city; how much more easily, in short, the most excruciating sorrows are pleasingly subdued on the fragrant border of a peaceful stream, than in the midst of those treacherous delights which occupy the courts of kings—all my wishes will be accomplished, and my happiness complete.

Retirement from the world may prove peculiarly beneficial at two periods of life: in youth, to acquire the rudiments of useful information, to lay the foundation of the character intended to be pursued, and to obtain that train of thought which is to guide us through life; in age, to cast a retrospective view on the course we have run; to reflect on the events we have observed, the vicissitudes we have experienced: to enjoy the flowers we have gathered on the way, and to congratulate ourselves upon the tempests we have survived. Lord Bolingbroke, in his "Idea of a Patriot King," says, there is not a more profound nor a finer observation in all lord Bacon's works, than the following: "We must choose betimes such virtuous objects as are proportioned to the means we have of pursuing them, and belong particularly to the stations we are in, and the duties of those stations. We must determine and fix our minds in such manner upon them, that the pursuit of them may become the business, and the attainment of them the end of our whole lives. Thus we shall imitate the great operations of nature, and not the feeble, slow, and imperfect operations of art. We must not proceed in forming the moral character, as a statuary proceeds in forming a statue, who works sometimes on the face, sometimes on one part, and sometimes on an other; but we must proceed, and it is in our power to proceed, as nature does in forming a flower, or any other of her productions; *rudimenta partium omnium simul parit et producit*: she throws out altogether, and at once, the whole system of every being, and the rudiments of all the parts."

It is, therefore, more especially to those youthful minds, who still remain susceptible of virtuous impressions, that I here pretend to point out the path which leads to true felicity. And if you acknowledge that I have enlightened your mind, corrected your manners, and tranquillized your heart, I shall congratulate myself on the success of my design, and think my labors richly rewarded.

Believe me, all ye amiable youths, from whose minds the artifices and gayeties of the world have not yet obliterated the precepts of a virtuous education; who are yet uninfected with its inglorious vanities; who, still ignorant of the tricks and blandishments of seduction, have preserved the desire to perform some glorious action, and retained the power to accomplish it; who, in the midst of feasting, dancing, and assemblies, feel an inclination to escape from their unsatisfactory delights; solitude will afford you a safe asylum. Let the voice of experience recommend you to cultivate a fondness for domestic pleasures, to incite and fortify your souls to noble deeds, to acquire that cool judgment and intrepid spirit which enables you to form correct estimates of the characters of mankind, and of the pleasures of society. But to accomplish this high end, you must turn your eyes from those trifling and insignificant examples which a degenerated race of men affords, and study the illustrious characters of the ancient Greeks, the Romans, and the Modern English. In what nation will you find more celebrated instances of human greatness? What people possesses more valor, courage, firmness, and knowledge; where do the arts and sciences shine with greater splendor, or with more useful effect? But do not deceive yourselves by a belief that you will acquire the character of an Englishman by wearing a cropped head of hair; no, you must pluck the roots of vice from your mind, destroy the seeds of weakness in your bosoms, and imitate the great examples of heroic virtue which that nation so frequently affords. It is an ardent love of liberty, undaunted courage, deep penetration, elevated sentiment, and well cultivated understanding, that constitute the British character; and not their cropped heads, half-boots, and round hats. It is virtue alone, and not dress or titles, that can ennoble or adorn the human character. Dress is an object too minute and trifling wholly to occupy a rational mind; and an illustrious descent is only advantageous as it renders the real merits of its immediate possessor more conspicuous. Never, however, lose sight of this important truth, that *no one can be truly great until he has gained a knowledge of himself*: a knowledge which can only be acquired by *occasional retirement*.

Chapter II
The influence of solitude upon the mind

The true value of liberty can only be conceived by minds that are free: slaves remain indolently contented in captivity. Men who have been long tossed upon the troubled ocean of life, and have learned by severe experience to entertain just notions of the world and its concerns, to examine every object with unclouded and impartial eyes, to walk erect in the strict and thorny paths of virtue, and to find their happiness in the reflections of an honest mind, alone are *free*.

The path of virtue, indeed, is devious, dark and dreary; but though it leads the traveller over hills of difficulty, it at length brings him into the delightful and extensive plains of permanent happiness and secure repose.

The love of solitude, when cultivated in the morn of life, elevates the mind to a noble independence; but to acquire the advantage which solitude is capable of affording, the mind must not be impelled to it by melancholy and discontent, but by a real distaste to the idle pleasures of the world, a rational contempt for the deceitful joys of life, and just apprehensions of being corrupted and seduced by its insinuating and destructive gayeties.

Many men have acquired and exercised in solitude that transcendent greatness of mind which defies events; and, like the majestic cedar, which braves the fury of the most violent tempest, have resisted, with heroic courage, the severest storms of fate.

Solitude, indeed, sometimes renders the mind in a slight degree arrogant and conceited; but these effects are easily removed by a judicious intercourse with mankind. Misanthropy, contempt of folly, and pride of spirit, are, in noble minds, changed by the maturity of age into dignity of character; and that fear of the opinion of the world which awed the weakness and inexperience of youth, is succeeded by firmness, and a high disdain of those false notions by which it was dismayed: the observations once so dreadful lose all their stings; the mind views objects not as they are, but as they ought to be; and, feeling a contempt for vice, rises into a noble enthusiasm for virtue, gaining from the conflict a rational experience and a compassionate feeling which never decay.

The science of the heart, indeed, with which youth should be familiarized as early as possible, is too frequently neglected. It removes the asperities and polishes the rough surfaces of the mind. This science is founded on that noble philosophy which regulates the characters of men; and operating more by love than by rigid precept, corrects the cold dictates of reason by the warm feelings of the heart; opens to view the dangers to which they are exposed; animates the dormant faculties of the mind, and prompts them to the practice of all the virtues.

Dion was educated in all the turpitude and servility of courts, accustomed to a life of softness and effeminacy, and, what is still worse, tainted by ostentation, luxury, and every species of vicious pleasure; but no sooner did he listen to the divine Plato, and acquire thereby a taste for that sublime philosophy which inculcates the practice of virtue, than his whole soul became deeply enamored of its charms. The same love of virtue with which Plato inspired the mind of Dion, may be silently, and almost imperceptibly infused by every tender mother into the mind of her child. Philosophy, from the lips of a wise and sensible woman, glides quietly, but with strong effect, into the mind through the feelings of the heart. Who is not fond of walking, even through the most rough and difficult paths, when conducted by the hand of love? What species of instruction can be more successful than soft lessons from a female tongue, dictated by a mind profound in understanding, and elevated in sentiment, where the heart feels all the affection that her precepts inspire? Oh! may every mother, so endowed, be blessed with a child who delights to listen in private to her edifying observations; who, with a book in his hand, loves to seek among the rocks some sequestered spot favorable to study; who when walking with his dogs and gun, frequently reclines under the friendly shade of some majestic tree, and contemplates the great and glorious characters which the pages of Plutarch present to his view, instead of toiling through the thickest of the surrounding woods hunting for game.

The wishes of a mother are accomplished when the silence and solitude of the forests seize and animate the mind of her loved child; when he begins to feel that he has seen sufficiently the pleasures of the world; when he begins to perceive that there are greater and more valued characters than noblemen or esquires, than ministers or kings; characters who enjoy a more elevated sense of pleasure than gaming tables and assemblies are capable of affording; who seek, at every interval of leisure, the shades of solitude with rapturous delight; whose minds have been inspired with a love of literature and philosophy from their earliest infancy; whose bosoms have glowed with a love of science through every subsequent period of their lives; and who, amidst the greatest calamities, are capable of banishing, by a secret charm, the deepest melancholy and most profound dejection.

The advantages of solitude to a mind that feels a real disgust at the tiresome intercourses of society, are inconceivable. Freed from the world, the veil which obscured the intellect suddenly falls, the clouds which dimmed the light of reason disappear, the painful burden which oppressed the soul is alleviated; we no longer wrestle with surrounding perils; the apprehension of danger vanishes; the sense of misfortune becomes softened; the dispensations of Providence no longer excite the murmur of discontent; and we enjoy the delightful pleasures of a calm, serene and happy mind. Patience and resignation follow and reside with a contented heart; every corroding care flies away on the wings of gayety; and on every side agreeable and interesting scenes present themselves to our view; the brilliant sun sinking behind the lofty mountains tinging their snow-crowned turrets with golden rays; the feathered choir hastening to seek within their mossy cells a soft, a silent, and secure repose; the shrill crowing of the amorous cock; the solemn and stately march of oxen returning from their daily toil, and the graceful paces of the generous steed. But, amidst the vicious pleasures of a great metropolis, where sense and truth are constantly despised, and integrity and conscience thrown aside as inconvenient and oppressive, the fairest forms of fancy are obscured, and the purest virtues of the heart corrupted.

But the first and most incontestable advantage of solitude is, that it accustoms the mind to think; the imagination becomes more vivid, and the memory more faithful, while the sense remains undisturbed, and no external object agitates the soul. Removed far from the tiresome tumults of public society, where a multitude of heterogeneous objects dance before our eyes and fill the mind with incoherent notions, we learn to fix our attention to a single subject, and to contemplate that alone. An author, whose works I could read with pleasure every hour of my life, says, "It is the power of attention which, in a great measure distinguishes the wise and great from the vulgar and trifling herd of men. The latter are accustomed to think, or rather to dream, without knowing the subject of their thoughts. In their unconnected rovings they pursue no end, they follow no track. Every thing floats loose and disjointed on the surface of their minds, like leaves scattered and blown about on the face of the waters."

The habit of thinking with steadiness and attention can only be acquired by avoiding the distraction which a multiplicity of objects always create; by turning our observation from external things, and seeking a situation in which our daily occupations are not perpetually shifting their course, and changing their direction.

Idleness and inattention soon destroy all the advantages of retirement; for the most dangerous passions, when the mind is not properly employed, rise into fermentation, and produce a variety of eccentric ideas and irregular desires. It is necessary, also, to elevate our thoughts above the mean consideration of sensual objects; the unincumbered mind then recalls all that it has read; all that has pleased the eye or delighted the ear; and reflecting on every idea which either observation, experience, or discourse, has produced, gains new information by every reflection, and conveys the purest pleasures to the soul. The intellect contemplates all the former scenes of life; views by anticipation those that are yet to come, and blends all ideas of past and future in the actual enjoyment of the present moment. To keep, however, the mental powers in proper tone, it is necessary to direct our attention invariably toward some noble and interesting study.

It may, perhaps, excite a smile, when I assert, that solitude is the only school in which the characters of men can be properly developed; but it must be recollected, that, although the materials of this study must be amassed in society, it is in solitude alone that we can apply them to their proper use. The world is the great scene of our observations; but to apply them with propriety to their respective objects is exclusively the work of solitude. It is admitted that a knowledge of the nature of man is necessary to our happiness; and therefore I cannot conceive how it is possible to call those characters malignant and misanthropic, who while they continue in the world, endeavor to discover even the faults, foibles and imperfections of human kind. The pursuit of this species of knowledge, which can only be gained by observation, is surely laudable, and not deserving the obloquy that has been cast on it. Do I, in my medical character, feel any malignity or hatred to the species, when I study the nature, and explore the secret causes of those weaknesses and disorders which are incidental to the human frame? When I examine the subject with the closest inspection, and point out for the general benefit, I hope, of mankind, as well as for my own satisfaction, all the frail and imperfect parts in the anatomy of the human body?

But a difference is supposed to exist between the observations which we are permitted to make upon the anatomy of the human body, and those which we assume respecting the philosophy of the mind. The physician, it is said, studies the maladies which are incidental to the human frame, to apply such remedies as particular occasion may require: but it is contended, that the moralist has a different end in view. This distinction, however, is certainly without foundation. A sensible and feeling philosopher views both the moral and physical defects of his fellow creatures with an equal degree of regret. Why do moralists shun mankind, by retiring into solitude, if it be not to avoid the contagion of those vices which they perceive so prevalent in the world, and which are not observed by those who are in the habit of seeing them daily indulged without censure or restraint? The mind, without doubt feels a considerable degree of pleasure in detecting the imperfections of human nature; and where that detection may prove beneficial to mankind, without doing an injury to any individual, to publish them to the world, to point out their qualities, to place them, by a luminous description before the eyes of men, is in my idea, a pleasure so far from being mischievous, that I rather think, and I trust I shall continue to think so even in the hour of death, it is the only real mode of discovering the machinations of the devil, and destroying the effects of his work. Solitude, therefore, as it tends to excite a disposition to think with effect, to direct the attention to proper objects, to strengthen observation, and to increase the natural sagacity of the mind, is the school in which a true knowledge of the human character is most likely to be acquired.

Bonnet, in an affecting passage of the preface to his celebrated work on the Nature of the Soul, relates the manner in which solitude rendered even his defect of sight advantageous to him. "Solitude," says he, "necessarily leads the mind to meditation. The circumstances in which I have hitherto lived, joined to the sorrows which have attended me for many years, and from which I am not yet released, induced me to seek in reflection those comforts which my unhappy condition rendered necessary; and my mind is now become my constant retreat: from the enjoyments it affords I derive pleasures which, like potent charms, dispel all my afflictions." At this period the virtuous Bonnet was almost blind. Another excellent character, of a different kind, who devotes his time to the education of youth, Pfeffel, at Colmar, supports himself under the affliction of total blindness in a manner equally noble and affecting, by a lifeless solitary indeed, but by the opportunities of frequent leisure which he employs in the study of philosophy, the recreations of poetry, and the exercises of humanity. There was formerly in Japan a college of blind persons, who, in all probability, were endued with quicker discernment than many members of more enlightened colleges. These sightless academicians devoted their time to the study of history, poetry, and music. The most celebrated traits in the annals of their country became the subject of their muse; and the harmony of their verses could only be excelled by the melody of their music. In reflecting upon the idleness and dissipation in which a number of solitary persons pass their time, we contemplate the conduct of these blind Japanese with the highest pleasure. The *mind's eye* opened and afforded them ample compensation for the loss of the corporeal organ. Light, life, and joy, flowed into their minds through surrounding darkness, and blessed them with high enjoyment of tranquil thought and innocent occupation.

Solitude teaches us to think, and thoughts become the principal spring of human actions; for the *actions* of men, it is truly said, are, nothing more than their *thoughts* embodied, and brought into substantial existence. The mind, therefore, has only to examine with candor and impartiality the idea which it feels the greatest inclination to pursue, in order to penetrate and expound the mystery of the human character; and he who has not been accustomed to self-examination, will upon such a scrutiny, frequently discover truths of extreme importance to his happiness, which the mists of worldly delusion had concealed totally from his view.

Liberty and leisure are all that an active mind requires in solitude. The moment such a character finds itself alone, all the energies of his soul put themselves into motion, and rise to a height incomparably greater than they could have reached under the impulse of a mind clogged and oppressed by the encumbrances of society. Even plodding authors, who only endeavor to improve the thoughts of others, and aim not at originality for themselves, derive such advantages from solitude, as to render them contented with their humble labors; but to superior minds, how exquisite are the pleasures they feel when solitude inspires the idea and facilitates the execution of works of virtue and public benefit! works which constantly irritate the passions of the foolish, and confound the guilty consciences of the wicked. The exuberance of a fine fertile imagination is chastened by the surrounding tranquility of solitude: all its diverging rays are concentrated to one certain point; and the mind exalted to such powerful energy, that whenever it is inclined to strike, the blow becomes tremendous and irresistible. Conscious of the extent and force of his powers, a character thus collected cannot be dismayed by legions of adversaries; and he waits, with judicious circumspection, to render sooner or later, complete justice to the enemies of virtue. The profligacy of the world, where vice usurps the seat of greatness, hypocrisy assumes the face of candor, and prejudice overpowers the voice of truth, must, indeed, sting his bosom with the keenest sensations of mortification and regret; but cast his philosophic eye over the disordered scene, he will separate what *ought to be indulged* from *what ought not to be endured*; and by a happy, well-timed stroke of satire from his pen, will destroy the bloom of vice, disappoint machinations of hipocrisy, and expose the fallacies on which prejudice is founded.

Truth unfolds her charms in solitude with superior splendor. A great and good man; Dr. Blair, of Edinburgh, says, "The great and the worthy, the pious and the virtuous, have ever been addicted to *serious retirement*. It is the characteristic of little and frivolous minds to be wholly occupied with the vulgar objects of life. These fill up their desires, and supply all the entertainment which their coarse apprehensions can relish. But a more refined and enlarged mind leaves the world behind it, feels a call for higher pleasures, and seeks them in retreat. The man of public spirit has recourse to it in order to reform plans for general good; the man of genius in order to dwell on his favorite themes; the philosopher to pursue his discoveries; and the saint to improve himself in grace."

Numa, the legislator of Rome, while he was only a private individual, retired on the death of Tatia, his beloved wife, into the deep forests of Aricia and wandered in solitary musings through the thickest groves and most sequestered shades. Superstition imputed his lonely propensity, not to disappointment, discontent, or hatred to mankind, but to a higher cause: a wish silently to communicate with some protecting deity. A rumor was circulated that the goddess Egeria, captivated by his virtues, had united herself to him in the sacred bonds of love, and by enlightening his mind, and storing it with superior wisdom, had led him to divine felicity. The Druids also, who dwelt among the rocks, in the woods, and in the most solitary places, are supposed to have instructed the infant nobility of their respective nations in wisdom and in eloquence, in the phenomena of nature, in astronomy, in the precepts of religion, and the mysteries of eternity. The profound wisdom thus bestowed on the characters of the Druids, although it was, like the story of Numa, the mere effects of imagination, discovers with what enthusiasm every age and country have revered those venerable characters who in the silence of the groves, and in the tranquillity of solitude, have devoted their time and talents to the improvement of the human mind, and the reformation of the species.

Genius frequently brings forth its finest fruit in solitude, merely by the exertion of its own intrinsic powers, unaided by the patronage of the great, the adulation of the multitude, or the hope of mercenary reward. Flanders, amidst all the horrors of civil discord, produced painters as rich in fame as they were poor in circumstances. The celebrated Correggio had so seldom been rewarded during his life, that the paltry payment of ten pistoles of German coin, and which he was obliged to travel as far as Parma, to receive, created in his mind a joy so excessive, that it caused his death. The self-approbation of conscious merit was the only recompense these great artists received; they painted with the hope of immortal fame; and posterity has done them justice.

Profound meditation in solitude and silence frequently exalts the mind above its natural tone, fires the imagination, and produces the most refined and sublime conceptions. The soul then tastes the purest and most refined delight, and almost loses the idea of existence in the intellectual pleasure it receives. The mind on every motion darts through space into eternity; and raised, in his free enjoyment of its powers by its own enthusiasm, strengthens itself in the habitude of contemplating the noblest subjects, and of adopting the most heroic pursuits. It was in a solitary retreat, amidst the shades of a lofty mountain near Byrmont, that the foundation of one of the most extraordinary achievements of the present age was laid. The king of Prussia, while on a visit to Spa, withdrew himself from the company, and walked in silent solitude amongst the most sequestered groves of this beautiful mountain, then adorned in all the rude luxuriance of nature, and to this day distinguished by the appellation of *"The Royal Mountain"*. [4] On this uninhabited spot, since become the seat of dissipation, the youthful monarch, it is said first formed the plan of conquering Silesia.

Solitude teaches with the happiest effect the important value of *time*, of which the indolent, having no conception, can form no estimate. A man who is ardently bent on employment, who is anxious not to live entirely in vain, never observes the rapid movements of a stop watch, the true image of transitory life, and most striking emblem of the flight of time, without alarm and apprehension. Social intercourse, when it tends to keep the mind and heart in a proper tone, when it contributes to enlarge the sphere of knowledge, or to banish corroding care, cannot, indeed, be considered a sacrifice of time. But where social intercourse, even when attended with these happy effects engages all our attention, turns the calmness of friendship into violence of love, transforms hours into minutes, and drives away all ideas, except those which the object of our affection inspires, year after year will roll unimproved away. Time properly employed never appears tedious; on the contrary, to him who is engaged in usefully discharging the duties of his station, according to the best of his ability, it is light, and pleasantly transitory.

A certain young prince, by the assistance of a number of domestics, seldom employs above five or six minutes in dressing. Of his carriage it would be incorrect to say he *goes* in it; for it *flies*. His table is superb and hospitable, but the pleasures of it are short and frugal. Princes, indeed, seem disposed to do every thing with rapidity. This royal youth who possesses extraordinary talents, and uncommon dignity of character, attends in his own person to every application, and affords satisfaction and delight in every interview. His domestic establishment engages his most scrupulous attention; and he employs seven hours every day without exception, throughout the year, in reading the best English, Italian, French, and German authors. It may therefore be truly said, that this prince is well acquainted with the value of time.

The hours which a man of the world throws idly away, are in solitude disposed of with profitable pleasure; and no pleasure can be more profitable than that which results from the judicious use of time. Men have many duties to perform: he, therefore, who wishes to discharge them honorably, will vigilantly seize the earliest opportunity, if he does not wish that any part of the passing moments should be torn like a useless page from the book of life. Useful employment stops the career of time, and prolongs our existence. To think and to work, is to live. Our ideas never flow with more rapidity and abundance, or with greater gayety, than in those hours which useful labor steals from idleness and dissipation. To employ our time with economy, we should frequently reflect how many hours escape from us against our inclination. A celebrated English author says, "When we have deducted all that is absorbed in sleep, all that is inevitably appropriated to the demands of nature, or irresistably engrossed by the tyranny of custom; all that is passed in regulating the superficial decorations of life, or is given up in the reciprocation of civility to the disposal of others; all that is torn from us by the violence of disease, or stolen imperceptibility away by lassitude and langor; we shall find that part of our duration very small of which we can truly call ourselves masters, or which we can spend wholly at our own choice. Many of our hours are lost in a rotation of petty cares, in a constant recurrence of the same employments, many of our provisions for ease or happiness are always exhausted by the present day, and a great part of our existence serves no other purpose than that of enabling us to enjoy the rest."

Time is never more misspent than while we declaim against the want of it; all our actions are then tinctured with peevishness. The yoke of life is certainly the least oppressive when we carry it with good humor; and in the shades of rural retirement, when we have once acquired a resolution to pass our hours with economy, sorrowful lamentations on the subject of time misspent, and business neglected, never torture the mind.

Solitude, indeed, may prove more dangerous than all the dissipation of the world, if the mind be not properly employed. Every man, from the monarch on the throne to the peasant in the cottage, should have a daily task, which he should feel it his duty to perform without delay. "*Carpe diem*," says Horace; and this recommendation will extend with equal propriety to every hour of our lives.

The voluptuous of every description, the votaries of Bacchus and the sons of Anacreon, exhort us to drive away corroding care, to promote incessant gaiety, and to enjoy the fleeting hours as they pass; and these precepts, when rightly understood, and properly applied, are founded in strong sense and sound reason; but they must not be understood or applied in the way these sensualists advise; they must not be consumed in drinking and debauchery; but employed in steadily advancing toward the accomplishment of the task which our respective duties require us to perform. "If," says Petrarch, "you feel any inclination to serve God, in which consists the highest felicities of our nature; if you are disposed to elevate the mind by the study of letters, which, next to religion, procures us the truest pleasures; if by your sentiments and writings, you are anxious to leave behind you something that will memorize your name with posterity; stop the rapid progress of time, and prolong the course of this uncertain life—fly, ah; fly, I beseech you, from the enjoyment of the *world*, and pass the few remaining days you have to live in ... *Solitude.*"

Solitude refines the taste, by affording the mind greater opportunities to call and select the beauties of those objects which engage its attention. There it depends entirely upon ourselves to make choice of those employments which afford the highest pleasure; to read those writings, and to encourage those reflections which tend mostly to purify the mind, and store it with the richest variety of images. The false notions which we so easily acquire in the world, by relying upon the sentiments of others, instead of consulting our own, are in solitude easily avoided. To be obliged constantly to say, "*I dare not think otherwise,*" is insupportable. Why, alas! will not men strive to form opinions of their own, rather than submit to be guided by the arbitrary dictates of others? If a work please me, of what importance is it to me whether the *beau monde* approve of it or not?—What information do I receive from you, ye cold and miserable critics?—Does your approbation make me feel whatever is truly noble, great and good, with higher relish or more refined delight?—How can I submit to the judgment of men who always examine hastily, and generally determine wrong?

Men of enlightened minds, who are capable of correctly distinguishing beauties from defects, whose bosoms feel the highest pleasure from the works of genius, and the severest pain from dullness and depravity, while they admire with enthusiasm, condemn with judgment and deliberation; and, retiring from the vulgar herd, either alone or in the society of selected friends, resign themselves to the delights of a tranquil intercourse with the illustrious sages of antiquity, and with those writers who have distinguished and adorned succeeding times.

Solitude, by enlarging the sphere of its information, by awakening a more lively curiosity, by relieving fatigue, and by promoting application, renders the mind more active, and multiplies the number of its ideas. A man who is well acquainted with all these advantages, has said, that, "by silent, solitary reflection, we exercise and strengthen all the powers of the mind. The many obstacles which render it difficult to pursue our path disperse and retire, and we return to a busy, social life, with more cheerfulness and content. The sphere of our understanding becomes enlarged by reflection; we have learned to survey more objects, and to behold them more intellectually together; we carry a clearer sight, a juster judgment, and firmer principles with us into the world in which we are to live and act; and are then more able, even in the midst of all its distractions, to preserve our attention, to think with accuracy, to determine with judgment, in a degree proportioned to the preparations we have made in the hours of retirement." Alas! in the ordinary commerce of the world, the curiosity of a rational mind soon decays, whilst in solitude it hourly augments. The researches of a finite being necessarily proceed by slow degrees. The mind links one proposition to another, joins experience with observation, and from the discovery of one truth proceeds in search of others. The astronomers who first observed the course of the planets, little imagined how important their discoveries would prove to the future interests and happiness of mankind. Attached by the spangled splendor of the firmament, and observing that the stars nightly changed their course, curiosity induced them to explore the cause of this phenomenon, and led them to pursue the road of science. It is thus that the soul, by silent activity, augments its powers; and a contemplative mind advances in knowledge in proportion as it investigates the various causes, the immediate effects, and the remote consequences of an established truth. Reason, indeed, by impeding the wings of the imagination, renders her flight less rapid, but it makes the object of attainment more sure. Drawn aside by the charms of fancy, the mind may construct new worlds; but they immediately burst, like airy bubbles formed of soap and water; while reason examines the materials of its projected fabric, and uses those only which are durable and good.

"The great art to learn much," says Locke, "is to undertake a little at a time." Dr. Johnson, the celebrated English writer, has very forcibly observed, that "all the performances of human art, at which we look with praise or wonder, are instances of the resistless force of perseverance: it is by this that the quarry becomes a pyramid, and that distant countries are united by canals. If a man was to compare the effect of a single stroke with the pick-axe, or of one impression of a spade, with the general design and last result, he would be overwhelmed with the sense of their disproportion; yet those petty operations, incessantly continued, in time surmount the greatest difficulties; and mountains are levelled, and oceans bounded by the slender force of human beings. It is therefore of the utmost importance that those who have any intention of deviating from the beaten roads of life, and acquiring a reputation superior to names hourly swept away by time among the refuse of fame, should add to their reason and their spirit the power of persisting in their purposes; acquire the art of sapping what they cannot batter; and the habit of vanquishing obstinate resistance by obstinate attacks."

It is activity of mind that gives life to the most dreary desert, converts the solitary cell into a social world, gives immortal fame to genius, and produces master-pieces of ingenuity to the artist. The mind feels a pleasure in the exercise of its powers proportioned to the difficulties it meets with, and the obstacles it has to surmount. When Apelles was reproached for having painted so few pictures, and for the incessant anxiety with which he retouched his works, he contented himself with this observation, "*I paint for posterity.*"

The inactivity of monastic solitude, the sterile tranquillity of the cloister, are ill suited to those who, after a serious preparation in retirement, and an assiduous examination of their own powers, feel a capacity and inclination to perform great and good actions for the benefit of mankind. Princes cannot live the lives of monks; statesmen are no longer sought for in monasteries and convents; generals are no longer chosen from the members of the church. Petrarch, therefore, very pertinently observes, "that solitude must not be inactive, nor leisure uselessly employed. A character indolent, slothful, languid, and detached from the affairs of life, must infallibly become melancholy and miserable. From such a being no good can be expected; he cannot pursue any useful science, or possess the faculties of a great man."

The rich and luxurious may claim an exclusive right to those pleasures which are capable of being purchased by pelf, in which the mind has no enjoyment, and which only afford a temporary relief to langor, by steeping the senses in forgetfulness; but in the precious pleasures of intellect, so easily accessible by all mankind, the great have no exclusive privilege; for such enjoyments are only to be procured by our own industry, by serious reflection, profound thought, and deep research; exertions which open hidden qualities to the mind, and lead it to the knowledge of truth, and to the contemplation of our physical and moral nature.

A Swiss preacher has in a German pulpit said, "The streams of mental pleasures, of which all men may equally partake, flow from one to the other; and that of which we have most frequently tasted, loses neither its flavor nor its virtues, but frequently acquires new charms, and conveys additional pleasure the oftener it is tasted. The subjects of these pleasures are as unbounded as the reign of truth, as extensive as the world, as unlimited as the divine perfections. Incorporeal pleasures, therefore, are much more durable than all others; they neither disappear with the light of the day, change with the external form of things, nor descend with our bodies to the tomb; but continue with us while we exist; accompany us under all the vicissitudes not only of our natural life, but of that which is to come; secure us in the darkness of the night, and compensate for all the miseries we are doomed to suffer."

Great and exalted minds, therefore, have always, even in the bustle of gaiety, or amidst the more agitated career of high ambition, preserved a taste for intellectual pleasures. Engaged in affairs of the most important consequence, notwithstanding the variety of objects by which their attention was distracted, they were still faithful to the muses, and fondly devoted their minds to works of genius. They disregarded the false notion, that reading and knowledge are useless to great men; and frequently condescended, without a blush, to become writers themselves.

Philip of Macedon, having invited Dionysius the younger to dine with him at Corinth, attempted to deride the father of his royal guest, because he had blended the characters of prince and poet, and had employed his leisure in writing odes and tragedies. "How could the king find leisure," said Philip, "to write those trifles?" "In those hours," answered Dionysius, "which you and I spend in drunkenness and debauchery."

Alexander who was passionately fond of reading and whilst the world resounded with his victories, whilst blood and carnage marked his progress, whilst he dragged captive monarchs at his chariot wheels, and marched with increasing ardor over smoking towns and desolated provinces in search of new objects of victory, felt during certain intervals, the langors of unemployed time; and lamenting that Asia afforded no books to amuse his leisure, he wrote to Harpalus to send him the works of Philistus, the tragedies of Euripides, Sophocles, Æschylus, and the dithyrambics of Thalestes.

Brutus, the avenger of the violated liberties of Rome, while serving in the army under Pompey, employed among books all the moments he could spare from the duties of his station; and was even thus employed during the awful night which preceded the celebrated battle of Pharsalia, by which the fate of the empire was decided. Oppressed by the excessive heat of the day, and by the preparatory arrangement of the army, which was encamped in the middle of summer on a marshy plain, he sought relief from the bath, and retired to his tent, where, whilst others were locked in the arms of sleep, or contemplating the event of the ensuing day, he employed himself until the morning dawned, in drawing a plan from the History of Polybius.

Cicero, who was more sensible of mental pleasures than any other character, says, in his oration for the poet Archias, "Why should I be ashamed to acknowledge pleasures like these, since for so many years the enjoyment of them has never prevented me from relieving the wants of others, or deprived me of the courage to attack vice and defend virtue? Who can justly blame, who can censure me, if, while others are pursuing the views of interest, gazing at festal shows and idle ceremonies, exploring new pleasures, engaged in midnight revels, in the distraction of gaming, the madness of intemperance, neither reposing the body, nor recreating the mind, I spend the recollective hours in a pleasing review of my past life, in dedicating my time to learning and the muses?"

Pliny the elder, full of the same spirit devoted every moment of his life to learning. A person read to him during his meals; and he never travelled without a book and a portable writing-desk by his side. He made extracts from every work he read; and scarcely conceiving himself alive while his faculties were absorbed in sleep, endeavored by his diligence, to double the duration of his existence.

Pliny the younger, read upon all occasions, whether riding, walking, or sitting, whenever a moment's leisure afforded him the opportunity; but he made it an invariable rule to prefer the discharge of the duties of his station to those occupations which he followed only as amusement. It was this disposition which so strongly inclined him to solitude and retirement. "Shall I never," exclaimed he in moments of vexation, "break the fetters by which I am restrained? Are they indissoluble? Alas! I have no hope of being gratified—every day brings new torments. No sooner is one duty performed than another succeeds. The chains of business become every hour more weighty and extensive."

The mind of Petrarch was always gloomy and dejected, except when he was reading, writing, or resigned to the agreeable illusions of poetry, upon the banks of some inspiring stream, among the romantic rocks and mountains, or the flower-enamelled vallies of the Alps. To avoid the loss of time during his travels, he constantly wrote at every inn where he stopped for refreshment. One of his friends, the bishop of Cavaillon, being alarmed lest the intense application with which he studied at Vaucluse might totally ruin a constitution already much impaired, requested of him one day the key of his library. Petrarch immediately gave it him without asking the reason of his request; when the good bishop, instantly locking up his books and writing-desk, said, "Petrarch, I hereby interdict you from the use of pen, ink, and paper, for the space of ten days." The sentence was severe; but the offender suppressed his feelings, and submitted to his fate. The first day of his exile from his favorite pursuits was tedious, the second accompanied with incessant headache, and the third brought on symptoms of an approaching fever. The bishop, observing his indisposition, kindly returned him the key, and restored him to his health.

The late earl of Chatham, on his entering into the world, was a cornet in a troop of horse dragoons. The regiment was quartered in a small village in England. The duties of his station were the first objects of his attention;

but the moment these were discharged, he retired into solitude during the remainder of the day, and devoted his mind to the study of history. Subject from his infancy to an hereditary gout, he endeavored to eradicate it by regularity and abstinence; and perhaps it was the feeble state of his health which first led him into retirement; but, however that may be, it was certainly in retirement that he had laid the foundation of that glory which he afterwards acquired. Characters of this description, it may be said, are no longer to be found; but in my opinion both the idea and assertion would be erroneous. Was the earl of Chatham inferior in greatness to a Roman? And will his son, who already, in the earliest stage of manhood, thunders forth his eloquence in the senate, like Demosthenes, and captivates like Pericles the hearts of all who hear him: who is now, even in the five-and-twentieth year of his age, dreaded abroad, and beloved at home, as prime minister of the British empire; ever think, or act under any circumstances with less greatness, than his illustrious father? What men have been, *man* may always be. Europe now produces characters as great as ever adorned a throne or commanded a field. Wisdom and virtue may exist, by proper cultivation, as well in public as in private life; and become as perfect in a crowded palace as in a solitary cottage.

Solitude will ultimately render the mind superior to all the vicissitudes and miseries of life. The man whose bosom neither riches, nor luxury, nor grandeur can render happy, may, with a book in his hand, forget all his torments under the friendly shade of every tree, and experience pleasures as infinite as they are varied, as pure as they are lasting, as lively as they are unfading, and as compatible with every public duty as they are contributary to private happiness. The highest public duty, indeed, is that of employing our faculties for the benefit of mankind, and can no where be so advantageously discharged as in solitude. To acquire a true notion of men and things, and boldly to announce our opinions to the world, is an indispensible obligation on every individual. The *press* is the channel through which writers diffuse the light of truth among *the people*, and display its radiance to the eyes of *the great.* Good writers inspire the mind with courage to think for itself; and the free communication of sentiments contributes to the improvement and imperfection of human reason. It is this love of liberty that leads men into solitude, where they may throw off the chains by which they are fettered in the world. It is this disposition to be free, that makes the man who thinks in solitude, boldly speak a language which, in the corrupted intercourse of society, he would not have dared openly to hazard. Courage is the companion of solitude. The man who does not fear to seek his comforts in the peaceful shades of retirement, looks with firmness on the pride and insolence of *the great*, and tears from the face of despotism the mask by which it is concealed.

His mind, enriched by knowledge, may defy the frowns of fortune, and see unmoved the various vicissitudes of life. When Demetrius had captured the city of Megara, and the property of the inhabitants had been entirely pillaged by the soldiers, he recollected that Stilpo, a philosopher of great reputation, who sought only the retirement and tranquility of a studious life, was among the number. Having sent for him, Demetrius asked him if he had lost any thing during the pillage? "No," replied the philosopher, *"my property is safe, for it exists only in my mind."*

Solitude encourages the disclosure of those sentiments and feelings which the manners of the world compel us to conceal. The mind there unburthens itself with ease and freedom. The pen, indeed, is not always taken up because we are alone; but if we are inclined to write, we ought to be alone. To cultivate philosophy, or court the muse with effect, the mind must be free from all embarrassment. The incessant cries of children, or the frequent intrusion of servants with messages of ceremony and cards of compliment, distract attention. An author, whether walking in the open air, seated in his closet, reclined under the shade of a spreading tree, or stretched upon a sofa, must be free to follow all the impulses of his mind, and indulge every bent and turn of his genius. To compose with success, he must feel an irresistible inclination, and be able to indulge his sentiments and emotions without obstacle or restraint. There are, indeed, minds possessed of a divine inspiration, which is capable of subduing every difficulty, and bearing down all opposition: and an author should suspend his work until he feels this secret call within his bosom, and watch for those propitious moments when the mind pours forth its ideas with energy, and the heart feels the subject with increasing warmth; for

> "... Nature's kindling breath
>
> Must fire the chosen genius; Nature's hand
>
> Must string his nerves and imp his eagle wings
>
> Impatient of the painful steep, to soar
>
> High as the summit; there to breath at large
>
> Ethereal air, with bards and sages old,
>
> Immortal sons of praise...."

Petrarch felt this sacred impulse when he tore himself from Avignon, the most vicious and corrupted city of the age, to which the pope had recently transferred the papal chair; and although still young, noble, ardent, honored by his holiness, respected by princes, courted by cardinals, he voluntarily quitted the splendid tumults of this brilliant court, and retired to the celebrated solitude of Vaucluse, at the distance of six leagues from Avignon, with only one servant to attend him, and no other possession than an humble cottage and its surrounding garden. Charmed with the natural beauties of this rural retreat, he adorned it with an excellent library, and dwelt, for many years, in wise tranquillity and rational repose, employing his leisure in completing and polishing his works: and producing more original compositions during this period than at any other of his life. But, although he here devoted much time and attention to his writings, it was long before he could be persuaded to make them public. Virgil calls the leisure he enjoyed at Naples, ignoble and obscure; but it was during this leisure that he wrote the Georgics, the most perfect of all his works, and which evince, in almost every line, that he wrote for immortality.

The suffrage of posterity, indeed, is a noble expectation, which every excellent and great writer cherishes with enthusiasm. An inferior mind contents itself with a more humble recompense, and sometimes obtains its due reward. But writers both great and good, must withdraw from the interruptions of society, and seeking the silence of the groves, and the shades, retire into their own minds: for every thing they perform, all that they produce, is the effect of solitude. To accomplish a work capable of existing through future ages, or deserving the approbation of contemporary sages, the love of solitude must entirely occupy their souls; for there the mind reviews and arranges, with the happiest effect, all the ideas and impressions it has gained in its observations in the world: it is there alone that the dart of satire can be truly sharpened against inveterate prejudices and infatuated opinions; it is there alone that the vices and follies of mankind present themselves accurately to the view of the moralist, and excite his ardent endeavors to correct and reform them. The hope of immortality is certainly the highest with which a great writer can possibly flatter his mind; but he must possess the comprehensive genius of a Bacon: think with the acuteness of Voltaire: compose with the ease and elegance of Rousseau; and, like them, produce master-pieces worthy of posterity in order to obtain it.

The love of fame, as well in the cottage as on the throne, or in the camp, stimulates the mind to the performance of those actions which are most likely to survive mortality and live beyond the grave, and which when achieved, render the evening of life as brilliant as its morning. "The praises (says Plutarch,) bestowed upon great and exalted minds, only spur on and rouse their emulation: like a rapid torrent, the glory which they have already acquired, hurries them irresistibly on to every thing that is great and noble.—They never consider themselves sufficiently rewarded. Their present actions are only pledges of what may be expected from them; and they would blush not to live faithful to their glory, and to render it still more illustrious by the noblest actions."

The ear which would be deaf to servile adulation and insipid compliment, will listen with pleasure to the enthusiasm with which Cicero exclaims, "Why should we dissemble what it is impossible for us to conceal? Why should we not be proud of confessing candidly that we all aspire to *fame*? The love of praise influences all mankind, and the greatest minds are the most susceptible of it. The philosophers who most preach up a contempt for fame, prefix their names to their works: and the very performances in which they deny ostentation, are evident proofs of their vanity and love of praise. Virtue requires no other reward for all the toils and dangers to which she exposes herself than that of fame and glory. Take away this flattering reward, and what would remain in the narrow career of life to prompt her exertions? If the mind could not launch into the prospect of futurity, or the operations of the soul were to be limited to the space that bounds those of the body, she would not weaken herself by constant fatigues, nor weary herself with continual watchings and anxieties; she would not think even life itself worthy of a struggle: but there lives in the breast of every good man a principle which unceasingly prompts and inspirits him to the pursuit of a fame beyond the present hour; a fame not commensurate to our mortal existence, but co-extensive with the latest posterity. Can we, who every day expose ourselves to dangers for our country, and have never passed one moment of our lives without anxiety or trouble, meanly think that all consciousness shall be buried with us in the grave? If the greatest men have been careful to preserve their busts and their statues, those images, not of their minds, but of their bodies, ought we not rather to transmit to posterity the resemblance of our wisdom and virtue? For my part, at least, I acknowledge, that in all my actions I conceived that I was disseminating and transmitting my fame to the remotest corners and the latest ages of the world. Whether, therefore, my consciousness of this shall cease in the grave, or, as some have thought, shall survive as a property of the soul, is of little importance. Of one thing I am certain, that at this instant I feel from the reflection a flattering hope and a delightful sensation."

This is the true enthusiasm with which preceptors should inspire the bosoms of their young pupils. Whoever shall be happy enough to light up this generous flame, and increase it by constant application, will see the object of his care voluntarily relinquish the pernicious pleasures of youth, enter with virtuous dignity on the stage of life, and add, by the performance of the noblest actions, new lustre to science, and brighter rays to glory. The desire of extending our fame by noble deeds, and of increasing the good opinion of mankind by a dignified conduct and real greatness of soul, confers advantages which neither illustrious birth, elevated rank, nor great fortune can bestow; and which, even on the throne, are only to be acquired by a life of exemplary virtue, and an anxious attention to the suffrages of posterity.

There is no character, indeed, more likely to acquire future fame than the satirist, who dares to point out and condemn the follies, the prejudices, and the growing vices of the age, in strong and nervous language. Works of this description, however they may fail to reform the prevailing manners of the times, will operate on succeeding generations, and extend their influence and reputation to the latest posterity. True greatness operates long after envy and malice have pursued the modest merit which produced it to the grave. O, Lavater! those base corrupted souls who only shine a moment, and are forever extinguished, will be forgotten, while the memory of thy name is carefully cherished, and thy virtues fondly beloved: thy foibles will be no longer remembered; and the qualities which distinguished and adorned thy character will alone be reviewed. The rich variety of thy language, the judgment with which thou hast boldly intended and created new expressions, the nervous brevity of thy style, and thy striking picture of human manners, will, as the author of "The Characters of German Poets and Prose writers" has predicted, extend the fame of thy "Fragments upon Physiognomy" to the remotest posterity. The accusation that Lavater, who was capable of developing such sublime truths, and of creating almost a new language, gave credit to the juggles of Gesner, will then be forgot; and he will enjoy the life after death, which Cicero seemed to hope for with so much enthusiasm.

Solitude, indeed, affords a pleasure to an author of which no one can deprive him, and which far exceeds all the honors of the world. He not only anticipates the effect his work will produce, but while it advances towards completion, feels the delicious enjoyment of those hours of serenity and composure which his labors procure. What continued and tranquil delight flows from this successive composition! Sorrows fly from this elegant occupation. O! I would not exchange one single hour of such tranquillity and content, for all those flattering illusions of public fame with which the mind of Tully was so incessantly intoxicated. A difficulty surmounted, a happy moment seized, a proposition elucidated, a sentence neatly and elegantly turned, or a thought happily expressed, are salutary and healing balms, counter-poisons to melancholy, and belong exclusively to a wise and well-formed solitude.

To enjoy himself without being dependant on the aid of others, to devote to employments not perhaps entirely useless, those hours which sorrow and chagrin would otherwise steal from the sum of life is the great advantage of an author; and with this advantage alone I am perfectly contented.

Solitude not only elevates the mind, but adds new strength to its powers. The man who has not courage to conquer the prejudices and despise the manners of the world, whose greatest dread is the imputation of singularity, who forms his opinion and regulates his conduct upon the judgment and actions of others, will certainly never possess sufficient strength of mind to devote himself to voluntary solitude; which, it has been well observed, is as necessary to give a just, solid, firm, and forcible tone to our thoughts, as an intercourse with the world is to give them richness, brilliancy, and just appropriation.

The mind, employed on noble and interesting subjects, disdains the indolence that stains the vacant breast. Enjoying freedom and tranquillity, the soul feels the extent of its energies with greater sensibility, and displays powers which it was before unconscious of possessing: the faculties sharpen; the mind becomes more clear, luminous, and extensive; the perception more distinct; the whole intellectual system, in short, exacts more from itself in the leisure of solitude than in the bustle of the world. But to produce these happy effects, solitude must not be reduced to a state of tranquil idleness and inactive ease, of mental numbness, or sensual stupor; it is not sufficient to be continually gazing out of a window with a vacant mind, or gravely walking up and down the study in a ragged *robe-de-chambre* and worn-out slippers; for the mere exterior of tranquillity cannot elevate or increase the activity of the soul, which must feel an eager desire to roam at large, before it can gain that delightful liberty and leisure, which at the same instant improves the understanding and corrects the imagination. The mind, indeed, is enabled, by the strength it acquires under the shades of retirement, to attack prejudices, and combat errors, with the unfailing prowess of the most athletic champion; for the more it examines into the nature of things, the closer it brings them to its view, and exposes, with unerring clearness, all the latent properties they possess. An intrepid and reflecting mind, when retired within itself, seizes with rapture on truth the moment it is discovered; looks round with a smile of pity and contempt on those who despise its charms; hears without dismay the invectives which envy and malice let loose against him; and nobly disdains the hue and cry which the ignorant multitude raise against him, the moment he elevates his hand to dart against them one of the strongest and invincible truths he has discovered in his retreat.

Solitude diminishes the variety of those troublesome passions which disturb the tranquillity of the human mind, by combining and forming a number of them into one great desire; for although it may certainly become dangerous to the passions, it may also, thanks to the dispensations of Providence! produce very salutary effects. If it disorder the mind, it is capable of effecting its cure. It extracts the various propensities of the human heart, and unites them into one. By this process we feel and learn not only the nature, but the extent, of all the passions which rise up against us like the angry waves of a disordered ocean, to overwhelm us in the abyss; but philosophy flies to our aid, divides their force, and, if we do not yield to them an easy victory, by neglecting all opposition to their attacks, virtue and self-denial bring gigantic reinforcements to our assistance, and ensure success. Virtue and resolution, in short, are equal to every conflict, the instant we learn that one passion is to be conquered by another.

The mind, exalted by the high and dignified sentiments it acquires by lonely meditation, becomes proud of its superiority, withdraws itself from every base and ignoble object, and avoids, with heroic virtue, the effect of dangerous society. A noble mind observes the sons of worldly pleasure mingling in scenes of riot and debauchery without being seduced; hears it in vain echoed from every side, that incontinence is among the first propensities of the human heart, and that every young man of fashion and spirit must as necessarily indulge his appetite for the fair sex, as the calls of hunger or of sleep. Such a mind perceives that libertinism and dissipation not only enervate youth, and render the feelings callous to the charms of virtue, and principles of honesty, but that it destroys every manly resolution, renders the heart timid, decreases exertion, damps the generous warmth and fine enthusiasm of the soul, and in the end, totally annihilates all its powers. The youth, therefore, who seriously wishes to sustain an honorable character on the theatre of life, must forever renounce the habits of indolence and luxury; and when he no longer impairs his intellectual faculties by debauchery, or renders it necessary to attempt the renovation of his languid and debilitated constitution by excess of wine and luxurious living, he will soon be relieved from the necessity of consuming whole mornings on horseback in a vain search of that health from change of scene which temperance and exercise would immediately bestow.

All men without exception, have something to learn; whatever may be the distinguished rank which they hold in society, they can never be truly great but by their personal merit. The more the faculties of the mind are exercised in the tranquillity of retirement, the more conspicuous they appear; and should the pleasures of debauchery be the ruling passion, learn, O young man! that nothing will so easily subdue it as an increasing emulation in great and virtuous actions, a hatred of idleness and frivolity, the study of the sciences, a frequent communication with your own heart, and that high and dignified spirit which views with disdain every thing that is vile and contemptible. This generous and high disdain of vice, this fond and ardent love of virtue, discloses itself in retirement with dignity and greatness, where the passion of high achievement operates with greater force than in any other situation. The same passion which carried Alexander into Asia, confined Diogenes to his tub. Heraclius descended from his throne to devote his mind to the search of truth. He who wishes to render his knowledge useful to mankind, must first study the world; not too intensely, or for any long duration, or with any fondness for its follies; for the follies of the world enervate and destroy the vigor of the mind. Cesar tore himself from the embraces of Cleopatra, and became the master of the world; while Antony took her as a mistress to his bosom, sunk indolently into her arms, and by his effeminacy lost not only his life, but the government of the Roman empire.

Solitude, indeed, inspires the mind with notions too refined and exalted for the level of common life. But a fondness for high conceptions, and a lively, ardent disposition, discovers to the votaries of solitude, the possibility of supporting themselves on heights which would derange the intellects of ordinary men. Every object that surrounds the solitary man enlarges the faculties of his mind, improves the feelings of his heart, elevates him above the condition of the species, and inspires his soul with views of immortality. Every day in the life of a man of the world seems as if he expected it would be the last of his existence. Solitude amply compensates for every privation, while the devotee of worldly pleasures conceives himself lost if he is deprived of visiting a fashionable assembly, of attending a favorite club, of seeing a new play, of patronizing a celebrated boxer, or of admiring some foreign novelty which the hand-bills of the day have announced.

I could never read without feeling the warmest emotions, the following passage of Plutarch; "I live," says he, "entirely upon history; and while I contemplate the pictures it presents to my view, my mind enjoys a rich repast from the representation of great and virtuous characters. If the actions of men produce some instances of vice, corruption, and dishonesty; I endeavor, nevertheless, to remove the impression, or to defeat its effect. My mind withdraws itself from the scene, and free from every ignoble passion, I attach myself to those high examples of virtue which are so agreeable and satisfactory, and which accord so completely with the genuine feelings of our nature."

The soul, winged by these sublime images, flies from the earth, mounts as it proceeds, and casts an eye of disdain on those surrounding clouds which, as they gravitate to the earth, would impede its flight. At a certain height the faculties of the mind expand, and the fibres of the heart dilate. It is, indeed, in the power of every man to perform more than he undertakes; and therefore it is both wise and praiseworthy to attempt every thing that is morally within our reach. How many dormant ideas may be awakened by exertion! and then, what a variety of early impressions, which were seemingly forgot, revive, and present themselves to our pens! We may always accomplish more than we conceive, provided passion fans the flame which the imagination has lighted; for life is insupportable when unanimated by the soft affections of the heart.

Solitude leads the mind to those sources from whence the grandest conceptions are most likely to flow. But alas! it is not in the power of every person to seize the advantages solitude bestows. Were every noble mind sensible of the extensive information, of the lofty and sublime ideas, of the exquisitely fine feelings which result from occasional retirement, they would frequently quit the world, even in the earliest periods of youth, to taste the sweets of solitude, and lay the foundation for a wise old age.

In conducting the low and petty affairs of life, common sense is certainly a more useful quality than even genius itself. Genius, indeed, or that fine enthusiasm which carries the mind into its highest sphere, is clogged and impeded in its ascent by the ordinary occupations of the world, and seldom regains its natural liberty and pristine vigor except in solitude. Minds anxious to reach the regions of philosophy and science have, indeed, no other means of rescuing themselves from the burden and thraldom of worldly affairs. Sickened and disgusted with the ridicule and obloquy they experience from an ignorant and presumptuous multitude, their faculties become, as it were, extinct, and mental exertion dies away; for the desire of fame, that great incentive to intellectual achievement, cannot long exist where merit is no longer rewarded by praise. But, remove such minds from the oppression of ignorance, of envy, of hatred, of malice; let them enjoy liberty and leisure; and with the assistance of pen, ink, and paper, they will soon take an ample revenge, and their productions excite the admiration of the world. How many excellent understandings remain in obscurity, merely on account of the possessor being condemned to follow worldly employments, in which little or no use of the mind is required, and which, for that reason, ought to be exclusively bestowed on the ignorant and illiterate vulgar! But this circumstance can seldom happen in solitude, where the mental faculties, enjoying their natural freedom, and roaming unconfined through all parts and properties of nature, fix on those pursuits most congenial to their powers, and most likely to carry them into their proper sphere.

The unwelcome reception which solitary men frequently meet with in the world, becomes, when properly considered, a source of enviable happiness; for to be universally beloved, would prove a great misfortune to him who is meditating in tranquillity the performance of some great and important work: every one would then be anxious to visit him, to solicit his visits in return, and to press for his attendance on all parties. But though philosophers are fortunately not in general the most favored guests in fashionable societies, they have the satisfaction to recollect, that it is not ordinary or common characters against whom the public hatred and disgust are excited. There is always something great in that man against whom the world exclaims, at whom every one throws a stone, and on whose character all attempt to fix a thousand crimes, without being able to prove one. The fate of a man of genius, who lives retired and unknown, is certainly more enviable: for he will then enjoy the pleasure of undisturbed retirement; and naturally imagining the multitude to be ignorant of his character, will not be surprised that they should continually misinterpret and pervert both his words and actions; or that the efforts of his friends to undeceive the public with respect to his merit should prove abortive.

Such was, in the mistaken view of the world, the fate of the celebrated count Schaumbourg Lippe, better known by the appellation of count de Buckebourg. No character, throughout Germany, was ever more traduced, or so little understood; and yet he was worthy of being enrolled among the highest names his age or country ever produced. When I first became acquainted with him, he lived in almost total privacy, quite retired from the world, on a small paternal farm, in the management of which consisted all his pleasure and employment. His exterior appearance was I confess, rather forbidding, and prevented superficial observers from perceiving the extraordinary endowments of his brilliant and capacious mind. The count de Lacy, formerly ambassador from the court of Madrid to Petersburgh, related to me during his residence at Hanover, that he led the Spanish army against the Portuguese at the time they were commanded by the count de Buckebourg; and that when the officers discovered him as they were reconnoitering the enemy with their glasses, the singularity of his appearance struck them so forcibly, that they immediately exclaimed, "Are the Portuguese commanded by Don Quixote?" The ambassador, however, who possessed a liberal mind, did justice in the highest terms, to the merit and good conduct of Buckebourg in Portugal; and praised, with enthusiastic admiration, the goodness of his mind, and the greatness of his character. Viewed at a distance, his appearance was certainly romantic; and his heroic countenance, his flowing hair, his tall and meagre figure, and particularly the extraordinary length of his visage, might, in truth, recall some idea of the celebrated knight of La Mancha: but, on a closer view, both his person and his manners dispelled the idea; for his features, full of fire and animation, announced the elevation, sagacity, penetration, kindness, virtue, and serenity of his soul; and the most sublime and heroic sentiments were as familiar and natural to his mind, as they were to the noblest characters of Greece and Rome.

The count was born in London, and possessed a disposition as whimsical as it was extraordinary. The anecdotes concerning him, which I heard from his relation, a German prince, are perhaps not generally known. Fond of contending with the English in every thing, he laid a wager that he would ride a horse from London to Edinburg backwards, that is, with the horse's head toward Edinburg, and the count's face toward London; and in this manner he actually rode through several counties in England, he travelled through the greater part of that kingdom on foot in the disguise of a common beggar. Being informed that part of the current of the Danube, above Regensberg, was so strong and rapid, that no one dared to swim across it; he made the attempt, and ventured so far that he nearly lost his life. A great statesman and profound philosopher at Hanover related to me, that during the war in which the count commanded the artillery in the army of prince Ferdinand of Brunswick against the French, he one day invited a number of Hanoverian officers to dine with him in his tent. While the company were in the highest state of festive mirth and gayety, a succession of cannon balls passed directly over the head of the tent. "The French cannot be far off!" exclaimed the officers. "Oh! I assure you," replied the count, "they are not near us;" and he begged the gentlemen would make themselves perfectly easy, resume their seats, and finish their dinner. Soon afterwards a cannon ball carried away the top of the tent, when the officers again rose precipitately from their seats, exclaiming, "The enemy are here!" "No, no," replied the count, "the enemy are not here; therefore I must request, gentlemen, that you will place yourselves at the table, and sit still, for you may rely on my word." The firing recommenced and the balls flew about in the same direction: the officers, however, remained fixed to their seats; and while they ate and drank in seeming tranquillity, whispered to each other their surmises and conjectures on this singular entertainment. At length the count, rising from his seat addressed the company in these words: "gentlemen, I was willing to convince you how well I can rely upon the officers of my artillery. I ordered them to fire, during the time we continued at dinner, at the pinnacle of the tent; and you have observed with what punctuality they obeyed my orders."

Characteristic traits of a man anxious to inure himself and those about him to arduous and difficult exploits will not be useless or unentertaining to curious and speculative minds. Being one day in company with the count at fort Wilhelmstein, by the side of a magazine of gunpowder, which he had placed in the room immediately under that in which he slept, I observed to him, that I should not be able to sleep very contentedly there during some of the hot nights of summer. The count, however, convinced me, though I do not now recollect by what means, that *the greatest danger and no danger, are one and the same thing.* When I first saw this extraordinary man, which was in the company of two officers, the one English the other Portuguese, he entertained me for two hours upon the physiology of Haller, whose works he knew by heart. The ensuing morning he insisted on my accompanying him in a little boat, which he rowed himself, to fort Wilhelmstein, built under his direction in the middle of the water, from plans, which he showed me of his own drawing. One Sunday, on the great parade at Pyrmont, surrounded by a vast concourse of men and women occupied in music, dancing, and gallantries, he entertained me during the course of two hours on the same spot, and with as much serenity if we had been alone, by detailing the various controversies respecting the existence of God, pointing out their defective parts and convincing me that he surpassed every writer in his knowledge of the subject. To prevent my escaping from this lecture, he held me fast the whole time by one of the buttons of my coat. At his country seat at Buckebourg, he showed me a large folio volume, in his own hand-writing, upon "The Art of defending a small town against a great force." The work was completely finished and intended as a present to the king of Portugal. There were many passages in it, which the count did me the favor to read relating to Swisserland, a country and people which he considered as invincible; pointing out to me not only all the important places they might occupy against an enemy, but discovering passes before unknown, and through which even a cat would scarce be able to crawl. I do not believe that any thing was ever written of higher importance to the interests of my country than this work; for it contains satisfactory answers to every objection that ever has or can be made. My friend M. Moyse Mendelsohm, to whom the cont read the preface to this work while he resided at Pyrmont, considered it as a master-piece of fine style and sound reasoning; for the count, when he pleased, wrote the French language with nearly as much elegance and purity as Voltaire: while in the German he was labored, perplexed, and diffuse. I must, however, add this in his praise, that, on his return from Portugal, he studied for many years under two of the most acute masters in Germany: first, Abbt; and afterwards Herder. Many persons who, from a closer intimacy and deeper penetration, have had greater opportunities of observing the conduct and character of this truly great and extraordinary man, relate of him a variety of anecdotes equally instructive and entertaining. I shall only add one observation more respecting his character, availing myself of the words of Shakspeare; the count Guilaume de Schaumbourg Lippe

"… carries no dagger.

He has a lean and hungry look;

… but he's not dangerous:

… he reads much:

He is a great observer: and he looks

Quite thro' the deeds of men. He loves no plays

… he hears no music;

Seldom he smiles, and smiles in such a sort,

As if he mock'd himself, and scorn'd his spirit,

That could be mov'd to smile at any thing."

Such was the character, always misunderstood, of this solitary man; and such a character might fairly indulge a contemptuous smile, on perceiving the mistaken sneers of an ignorant multitude. But what must be the shame and confusion of the partial judges of mankind, when they behold the monument which the great Mendelsohm has raised to his memory; and the faithful history of his life and manners which a young author is about to publish at Hanover; the profound sentiments, the elegant style, the truth, and the sincerity of which will be discovered and acknowledged by impartial posterity?

The men who, as I have frequently observed, are disposed to ridicule this illustrious character on account of his long visage, his flowing hair, his enormous hat, or his little sword, might be pardoned, if, like him, they were philosophers or heroes. The mind of the count, however, was too exalted to be moved by their insulting taunts, and he never smiled upon the world, or upon men, either with spleen or with contempt. Feeling no hatred, indulging no misanthropy, his looks beamed kindness on all around him; and he enjoyed with dignified composure the tranquillity of his rural retreat in the middle of a thick forest, either alone or in the company of a fond and virtuous wife, whose death so sensibly afflicted even his firm and constant mind, that it brought him almost to an untimely grave. The people of Athens laughed at Themistocles, and openly reviled him even in the streets, because he was ignorant of the manners of the world, the *ton* of good company, and that accomplishment which is called good breeding. He retorted, however, upon these ignorant railers with the keenest asperity: "It is true," said he, "I never play upon the lute; but I know how to raise a small and inconsiderable city to greatness and to glory."

Solitude and philosophy may inspire sentiments which appear ludicrous to the eye of worldly folly, but they banish all light and insignificant ideas, and prepare the mind for the grandest and most sublime conceptions. Those who are in the habit of studying great and exalted characters, of cultivating refined and elevated sentiments, unavoidably contract a singularity of manners which may furnish ample materials for ridicule. Romantic characters always view things differently from what they really are or can be; and the habit of invariably contemplating the sublime and beautiful, renders them, in the eyes of the weak and wicked, insipid and unsupportable. Men of this disposition always acquire a high and dignified demeanor, which shocks the feelings of the vulgar; but it is not on that account the less meritorious. Certain Indian philosophers annually quitted their solitude to visit the palace of their sovereign, where each of them, in his turn, delivered his advice upon the government of the state, and upon the changes and limitations which might be made in the laws; but he who three successive times communicated false or unimportant observations, lost for one year, the privilege of appearing in the presence-chamber. This practice is well calculated to prevent the mind from growing romantic: but there are many philosophers of a different description, who if they had the same opportunity, would not meet with better success.

Plotinus requested the emperor Gallienus to confer on him a small city in Campania, and the territory appendant to it, promising to retire to it with his friends and followers, and to realise in the government of it the Republic of Plato. It happened then, however, as it frequently happens now in many courts, to philosophers much less chimerical than Plotinus; the statesmen laughed at the proposal, and told the emperor that the philosopher was a fool, in whose mind even experience had produced no effect.

The history of the greatness and virtues of the ancients operate in solitude with the happiest effect. Sparks of that bright flame which warmed the bosoms of the great and good, frequently kindled unexpected fires. A lady in the country, whose health was impaired by nervous affections, was advised to read with attention the history of the Greek and Roman empires. At the expiration of three months she wrote to me in the following terms: "You have inspired my mind with a veneration for the virtues of the ancients. What are the buzzing race of the present day, when compared with those noble characters? History heretofore was not my favorite study: but now I live only in its pages. While I read of the transactions of Greece and Rome, I wish to become an actor in the scenes. It has not only opened to me an inexhaustible source of pleasure, but it has restored me to health. I could not have believed that my library contained so inestimable a treasure: my books will now prove more valuable to me than all the fortune I possess; in the course of six months you will no longer be troubled with my complaints. Plutarch is more delightful to me than the charms of dress, the triumphs of coquetry, or the sentimental effusions which lovers address to those mistresses who are inclined to be all heart; and with whom satan plays tricks of love with the same address as a dilettante plays tricks of music on the violin." This lady, who is really learned, no longer fills her letters with the transactions of her kitchen and poultry yard; she has recovered her health; and will experience hereafter, I conjecture, as much pleasure among her hens and chickens, as she did before from the pages of Plutarch.

But although the immediate effects of such writings cannot be constantly perceived, except in solitude, or in the society of select friends, yet they may remotely be productive of the happiest consequences. The mind of a man of genius, during his solitary walks, is crowded with a variety of ideas, which, on being disclosed, would appear ridiculous to the common herd of mankind: a period, however, arrives, at which they lead men to the performance of actions worthy of immortality. The national songs composed by that ardent genius Lavater, appeared at a moment when the republic was in a declining state, and the temper of the times unfavorable to their reception. The Schintzuach society, by whose persuasion they had been written, had given some offence to the French ambassador; and from that time all the measures which the members adopted were decried with the most factious virulence in every quarter. Even the great Haller, who had been refused admission, considering them as disciples of Rousseau, whom he hated; and as enemies to orthodoxy, which he loved; pointed his epigrams against them in every letter I received from him; and the committee for the reformation of literature at Zurich expressly prohibited the publication of these excellent lyric compositions, on the curious pretence, that it was dangerous and improper to stir up a dunghill. No poet of Greece, however, ever wrote with more fire and force in favor of his country than Lavater did in favor of the liberties of Swisserland. I have heard children chaunt these songs with patriotic enthusiasm; and seen the finest eyes filled with tears of rapture while their ears listened to the singers. Joy glowed in the breasts of the Swiss peasants to whom they were sung: their muscles swelled, and the blood inflamed their cheeks. Fathers have, within my own knowledge, carried their infant children to the chapel of the celebrated William Tell, to join in full chorus the song which Lavater composed upon the merits of that great man. I have myself made the rocks re-echo to my voice, by singing these songs to the music which the feelings of my heart composed for them while wandering over the fields, and climbing among the famous mountains where those heroes, the ancestors of our race, signalized themselves by their immortal valor. I fancied that I saw them still armed with their knotted clubs, breaking to pieces the crowned helmets of Germany; and although inferior in numbers, forcing the proud nobility to seek their safety by a precipitate and ignominious flight. These, it may be said, are romantic notions, and can only please solitary and recluse men, who see things differently from the rest of the world. But great ideas sometimes now make their way in spite of the most obstinate opposition, and operating, particularly in republics, by insensible degrees, sow the seeds of those principles and true opinions, which, as they arrive to maturity, prove so efficacious in times of political contest and public commotion.

Solitude, therefore, by instilling high sentiments of human nature, and heroic resolutions in defence of its just privileges, unites all the qualities which are necessary to raise the soul and fortify the character, and forms an ample shield against the shafts of envy, hatred or malice. Resolved to think and to act, upon every occasion in opposition to the sentiments of narrow minds, the solitary man attends to all the various opinions he meets with, but is astonished at none. Without being ungrateful for the just and rational esteem his intimate friends bestow upon him; remembering, too, that friends, always partial, and inclined to judge too favorably, frequently, like enemies, suffer their feelings to carry them too far; he boldly calls upon the public voice to announce his character to the world at large: displays his just pretensions before this impartial tribunal, and demands that justice which is due.

But solitude, although it exalts the sentiments, is generally conceived to render the mind unfit for business: this, however, is, in my opinion, a great mistake. To avoid tottering through the walks of public duty, it must be of great utility to have acquired a firm step, by exercising the mind in solitude on those subjects which are likely to occur in public life. The love of truth is best preserved in solitude, and virtue there acquires greater consistency: but I confess truth is not always convenient in business nor the rigid exercise of virtue propitious to worldly success.

The *great* and the *good* however, of every clime, revere the simplicity of manners, and the singleness of heart, which solitude produces. It was these inestimable qualities which during the fury of the war between England and France, obtained the philosophic Jean Andre de Luc the reception he met with at the court of Versailles; and inspired the breast of the virtuous, the immortal de Vergennes with the desire to reclaim, by the mild precepts of a philosopher, the refractory citizens of Geneva, which all his remonstrances, as prime minister of France, had been unable to effect. De Luc, at the request of Vergennes made the attempt, but failed of success; and France, as it is well known, was obliged to send an army to subdue the Genevese. It was upon his favorite mountains that this amiable philosopher acquired that simplicity of manners, which he still preserves amidst all the luxuries and seductions of London; where he endures with firmness all the wants, refuses all the indulgences, and subdues all the desires of social life. While he resided at Hanover, I only remarked one single instance of luxury in which he indulged himself; when any thing vexed his mind, he chewed a small morsel of sugar, of which he always carried a small supply in his pocket.

Solitude not only creates simplicity of manners, but prepares and strengthens the faculties for the toils of busy life. Fostered in the bosom of retirement, the mind becomes more active in the world and its concerns, and retires again into tranquillity to repose itself, and prepare for new conflicts. Pericles, Phocion, and Epaminondas, laid the foundation of all their greatness in solitude, and acquired there rudiments, which all the language of the schools cannot teach—the rudiments of their future lives and actions. Pericles, while preparing his mind for any important object, never appeared in public, but immediately refrained from feasting, assemblies, and every species of entertainment; and during the whole time that he administered the affairs of the republic, he only went once to sup with a friend, and left him at an early hour. Phocion immediately resigned himself to the study of philosophy: not from the ostentatious motive of being called a *wise man*, but to enable himself to conduct the business of the state with greater resolution and effect. Epaminondas, who had passed his whole life in the delights of literature, and in the improvement of his mind, astonished the Thebans by the military skill and dexterity which he all at once displayed at the battles of Mantinea and Leuctra, in the first of which he rescued his friend Pelopidas: but it was owing to the frugal use he made of his time, to the attention with which he devoted his mind to every pursuit he adopted, and to that solitude which his relinquishment of every public employment afforded him. His countrymen, however, forced him to abandon his retreat, gave him the absolute command of the army; and by his military skill, he saved the republic.

Petrarch, also a character I never contemplate but with increasing sensibility, formed his mind, and rendered it capable of transacting the most complicated political affairs, by the habit he acquired in solitude. He was, indeed, what persons frequently become in solitude, choleric, satirical, and petulant: and has been severely reproached with having drawn the manners of his age with too harsh and sombrous a pencil, particularly the scenes of infamy which were transacted at the court of Avignon, under the pontificate of Clement VI.; but he was a perfect master of the human heart, knew how to manage the passions with uncommon dexterity, and to turn them directly to his purposes. The abbe de Sades, the best historian of his life, says, "he is scarcely known, except as a tender and elegant poet, who loved with ardor, and sung, in all the harmony of verse, the charms of his mistress." But was this in reality the whole of his character?—Certainly not. Literature, long buried in the ruins of barbarity, owes the highest obligations to his pen; he rescued some of the finest works of antiquity from dust and rottenness; and many of those precious treasures of learning, which have since contributed to delight and instruct mankind, were discovered by his industry, corrected by his learning and sagacity, and multiplied in accurate copies at his expense. He was the great restorer of elegant writing and true taste; and by his own compositions, equal to any that ancient Rome, previous to its subjugation, produced, purified the public mind, reformed the manners of the age, and extirpated the prejudices of the times. Pursuing his studies with unremitting firmness to the hour of his death, his last work surpassed all that had preceded it. But he was not only a tender lover, an elegant poet, and a correct and classical historian, but an able statesman also, to whom the most celebrated sovereigns of his age confided every difficult negotiation, and consulted in their most important concerns. He possessed, in the fourteenth century, a degree of fame, credit, and influence, which no man of the present day, however learned, has ever acquired. Three popes, an emperor, a sovereign of France, a king of Naples, a crowd of cardinals, the greatest princes, and the most illustrious nobility of Italy, cultivated his friendship, and solicited his correspondence. In the several capacities of statesman, minister, and ambassador, he was employed in transacting the greatest affairs, and by that means was enabled to acquire and disclose the most useful and important truths. These high advantages he owed entirely to solitude, with the nature of which as he was better acquainted than any other person, so he cherished it with greater fondness, and resounded its praise with higher energy; and at length preferred his leisure and liberty to all the enjoyments of the world. Love, to which he had consecrated the prime of life, appeared, indeed, for a long time, to enervate his mind; but suddenly abandoning the soft and effeminate style in which he breathed his sighs at Laura's feet, he addressed kings, emperors, and popes, with manly boldness, and with that confidence which splendid talents and a high reputation always inspires. In an elegant oration, worthy of Demosthenes and Cicero, he endeavored to compose the jarring interests of Italy; and exhorted the contending powers to destroy with their confederated arms, the barbarians, those common enemies of their country, who were ravaging its very bosom, and preying on its vitals. The enterprises of Rienzi, who seemed like an agent sent from heaven to restore the decayed metropolis of the Roman empire to its former splendor, were suggested, encouraged, directed, and supported by his abilities. A timid emperor was roused by his eloquence to invade Italy, and induced to seize upon the reins of government, as successor to the Cesars. The pope, by his advice, removed *the holy chair*, which had been transported to the borders of the Rhine, and replaced it on the banks of the

Tiber; and at a moment even when he confessed, in one of his letters, that his mind was distracted with vexation, his heart torn with love, and his whole soul disgusted with men and measures. Pope Clement VI, confided to his negotiation an affair of great difficulty at the court of Naples, in which he succeeded to the highest satisfaction of his employer. His residence at courts, indeed, had rendered him ambitious, busy, and enterprising; and he candidly acknowledged, that he felt a pleasure on perceiving a hermit, accustomed to dwell only in woods, and to saunter over plains, running through the magnificent palaces of cardinals with a crowd of courtiers in his suite. When John Visconti, archbishop and prince of Milan, and sovereign of Lombardy, who united the finest talents with ambition so insatiable, that it threatened to swallow up all Italy, had the happiness to fix Petrarch in his interests, by inducing him to accept of a seat in his council, the friends of the philosopher whispered one among another, "This stern republican who breathed no sentiments but those of liberty and independence; this untamed bull, who roared so loud at the slightest shadow of the yoke; who could endure no fetters but those of love, and who even felt those too heavy: who has refused the first offices at the court of Rome, because he disdained to wear golden chains; has at length submitted to be shackled by the tyrant of Italy; and this great apostle of solitude, who could no longer live except in the tranquillity of the groves, now contentedly resides amidst the tumults of Milan." "My friends," replied Petrarch, "have reason to arraign my conduct. Man has not a greater enemy than himself. I acted against my taste and inclination. Alas! through the whole course of our lives, we do those things which we ought not to have done, and leave undone what most we wish to do." But Petrarch might have told his friends, "I was willing to convince you how much a mind, long exercised in solitude, can perform when engaged in the business of the world; how much a previous retirement enables a man to transact the affairs of public life with ease, firmness, dignity and effect."

The courage which is necessary to combat the prejudices of the multitude, is only to be acquired by a contempt of the frivolous transactions of the world, and, of course is seldom possessed, except by solitary men. Worldly pursuits, so far from adding strength to the mind, only weaken it; in like manner as any particular enjoyment too frequently repeated, dulls the edge of the appetite for every pleasure. How often do the best contrived and most excellent schemes fail, merely for want of sufficient courage to surmount the difficulty which attend their execution!—How many happy thoughts have been stifled in their birth, from an apprehension that they were too bold to be indulged!

An idea has prevailed, that truth can only be freely and boldly spoken under a republican form of government; but this idea is certainly without foundation. It is true, that in aristocracies, as well as under a more open form of government, where a single demagogue unfortunately possesses the sovereign power, common sense is too frequently construed into public offence. Where this absurdity exists, the mind must be timid, and the people in consequence deprived of their liberty. In a monarchy every offence is punished by the sword of justice; but in a republic, punishments are inflicted by prejudices, passions, and state necessity. The first maxim which, under a republican form of government, parents endeavor to instil into the minds of their children, is, *not to make enemies*; and I remember, when I was very young, replying to this sage counsel, "My dear mother, do you not know that he who has no enemies is a poor man?" In a republic the citizens are under the authority and jealous observation of a multitude of sovereigns; while in a monarchy the reigning prince is the only man whom his subjects are bound to obey. The idea of living under the control of a number of masters intimidates the mind; whereas love and confidence in *one* alone, raises the spirits and renders the people happy.

But in all countries, and under every form of government, the rational man, who renounces the useless conversation of the world, who lives a retired life, and who, independently of all that he sees, of all that he hears, forms his notions in tranquillity, by an intercourse with the heroes of Greece, of Rome, and of Great Britain, will acquire a steady and uniform character, obtain a noble style of thinking, and rise superior to every vulgar prejudice.

These are the observations I had to make respecting the influence of occasional solitude upon the mind. They disclose my real sentiments on this subject: many of them, perhaps, undigested, and many more certainly not well expressed. But I shall console myself for these defects, if this chapter affords only a glimpse of those advantages, which, I am persuaded, a rational solitude is capable of affording to the minds and manners of men; and if that which follows shall excite a lively sensation of the true, noble, and elevated pleasures retirement is capable of producing by a tranquil and feeling contemplation of nature, and by an exquisite sensibility for every thing that is good and fair.

Chapter III
Influence of Solitude upon the Heart

The highest happiness which is capable of being enjoyed in this world, consists in *peace of mind*. The wise mortal who renounces the tumults of the world, restrains his desires and inclinations, resigns himself to the dispensations of his Creator, and looks with an eye of pity on the frailties of his fellow creatures; whose greatest pleasure is to listen among the rocks to the soft murmurs of a cascade; to inhale, as he walks along the plains, the refreshing breezes of the zephyrs; and to dwell in the surrounding woods, on the melodious accents of the aerial choristers; may, by the simple feelings of his heart, obtain this invaluable blessing.

To taste the charms of retirement, it is not necessary to divest the heart of its emotions. The world may be renounced without renouncing the enjoyment which the tear of sensibility is capable of affording. But to render the heart susceptible of this felicity, the mind must be able to admire with equal pleasure nature in her sublimest beauties, and in the modest flower that decks the vallies; to enjoy at the same time that harmonious combination of parts which expands the soul, and those detached portions of the whole which present the softest and most agreeable images to the mind. Nor are these enjoyments exclusively reserved for those strong and energetic bosoms whose sensations are as lively as they are delicate, and in which, for that reason, the good and the bad make the same impression: the purest happiness, the most enchanting tranquillity, are also granted to men of colder feelings, and whose imaginations are less bold and lively; but to such characters the portraits must not be so highly colored, nor the tints so sharp; for as the bad strikes them less, so also they are less susceptible of livelier impressions.

The high enjoyments which the heart feels in solitude are derived from the imagination. The touching aspect of delightful nature, the variegated verdure of the forests, the resounding echoes of an impetuous torrent, the soft agitation of the foliage, the warblings of the tenants of the groves, the beautiful scenery of a rich and extensive country, and all those objects which compose an agreeable landscape, take such complete possession of the soul, and so entirely absorb our faculties, that the sentiments of the mind are by the charms of the imagination instantly converted into sensations of the heart, and the softest emotions give birth to the most virtuous and worthy sentiments. But to enable the imagination thus to render every object fascinating and delightful, it must act with freedom, and dwell amidst surrounding tranquillity. Oh! how easy is it to renounce noisy pleasures and tumultuous assemblies for the enjoyment of that philosophic melancholy which solitude inspires!

Religious awe and rapturous delight are alternately excited by the deep gloom of forests, by the tremendous height of broken rocks, and by the multiplicity of majestic and sublime objects which are combined within the site of a delightful and extensive prospect. The most painful sensations immediately yield to the serious, soft, and solitary reveries to which the surrounding tranquillity invites the mind; while the vast and awful silence of nature exhibits the happy contrast between simplicity and grandeur; and as our feelings become more exquisite, so our admiration becomes more intense, and our pleasures more complete.

I had been for many years familiar with all that nature is capable of producing in her sublimest works, when I first saw a garden in the vicinity of Hanover, and another upon a much larger scale at Marienwerder, about three miles distant, cultivated in the English style of rural ornament. I was not then apprized of the extent of that art which sports with the most ungrateful soil, and, by a new species of creation, converts barren mountains into fertile fields and smiling landscapes. This magic art makes an astonishing impression on the mind, and captivates every heart, not insensible to the delightful charms of cultivated nature. I cannot recollect without shedding tears of gratitude and joy, a single day of this early part of my residence in Hanover, when, torn from the bosom of my country, from the embraces of my family, and from every thing that I held dear in life, my mind, on entering the little garden of my deceased friend, M. de Hinuber, near Hanover, immediately revived, and I forgot, for the moment, both my country and my grief. The charm was new to me. I had no conception that it was possible, upon so small a plot of ground, to introduce at once the enchanting variety and the noble simplicity of nature. But I was then convinced, that her aspect alone is sufficient, at first view, to heal the wounded feelings of the heart, to fill the bosom with the highest luxury, and to create those sentiments in the mind, which can, of all others, render life desirable.

This new re-union of art and nature, which was not invented in China, but in England, is founded upon a rational and refined taste for the beauties of nature, confirmed by experience, and by the sentiments which a chaste fancy reflects on a feeling heart.

But in the gardens I have before mentioned, every point of view raises the soul to heaven, and affords the mind sublime delight; every bank presents a new and varied scene, which fills the heart with joy: nor, while I feel the sensation which such scenes inspire, will I suffer my delight to be diminished by discussing whether the arrangement might have been made in a better way, or permit the dull rules of cold and senseless masters to destroy my pleasure. Scenes of serenity, whether created by tasteful art, or by the cunning hand of nature, always bestow, as a gift from the imagination, tranquillity to the heart. While a soft silence breathes around me, every object is pleasant to my view; rural scenery fixes my attention, and dissipates the grief that lies heavy at my heart; the loveliness of solitude enchants me, and, subduing every vexation, inspires my soul with benevolence, gratitude, and content. I return thanks to my Creator for endowing me with an imagination, which, though it has frequently caused the trouble of my life, occasionally leads me, in the hour of my retirement, to some friendly rock, on which I can climb, and contemplate with greater composure the tempests I have escaped.

There are, indeed, many Anglicised gardens in Germany, laid out so whimsically absurd, as to excite no other emotions than those of laughter or disgust. How extremely ridiculous is it to see a forest of poplars, scarcely sufficient to supply a chamber stove with fuel for a week; mere molehills dignified with the name of mountains; caves and aviaries, in which tame and savage animals, birds and amphibious creatures, are attempted to be represented in their native grandeur; bridges, of various kinds, thrown across rivers, which a couple of ducks would drink dry; and wooden fishes swimming in canals, which the pump every morning supplies with water! These unnatural beauties are incapable of affording any pleasure to the imagination.

A celebrated English writer has said, that "solitude, on the first view of it, inspires the mind with terror, because every thing that brings with it the idea of privation is terrific, and therefore sublime like space, darkness, and silence."

The species of greatness which results from the idea of infinity, can only be rendered delightful by being viewed at a proper distance. The Alps, in Swisserland, and particularly near the canton of Berne, appear inconceivably majestic; but on a near approach, they excite ideas certainly sublime, yet mingled with a degree of terror. The eye, on beholding those immense and enormous masses piled one upon the other, forming one vast and uninterrupted chain of mountains, and rearing their lofty summits to the skies, conveys to the heart the most rapturous delight, while the succession of soft and lively shades which they throw around the scene, tempers the impression, and renders the view as agreeable as it is sublime. On the contrary, no feeling heart can on a close view, behold this prodigious wall of rocks without experiencing involuntary trembling. The mind contemplates with affright their eternal snows, their steep ascents, their dark caverns, the torrents which precipitate themselves with deafening clamor from their summits, the black forests of firs that overhang their sides, and the enormous fragments of rocks which time and tempests have torn away. How my heart thrilled when I first climbed through a steep and narrow track upon these sublime deserts, discovering every step I made, new mountains rising over my head, while upon the least stumble, death menaced me in a thousand shapes below! But the imagination immediately kindles when you perceive yourself in the midst of this grand scene of nature, and reflect from these heights on the weakness of human power, and the imbecility of the greatest monarchs!

The history of Swisserland evinces, that the natives of these mountains are not a degenerate race of men, and that their sentiments are as generous as their feelings are warm. Bold and spirited by nature, the liberty they enjoy gives wings to their souls, and they trample tyrants and tyranny under their feet. Some of the inhabitants of Swisserland, indeed, are not perfectly free; though they all possess notions of liberty, love their country, and return thanks to the Almighty for that happy tranquillity which permits each individual to live quietly under his vine, and enjoy the shade of his fig-tree; but the most pure and genuine liberty is always to be found among the inhabitants of these stupendous mountains.

The Alps in Swisserland are inhabited by a race of men sometimes unsocial, but always good and generous. The hardy and robust characters given to them by the severity of their climate, is softened by pastoral life. It is said by an English writer, that he who has never heard a storm in the Alps, can form no idea of the continuity of the lightning, the rolling and the burst of the thunder which roars round the horizon of these immense mountains; and the people never enjoying better habitations than their own cabins, nor seeing any other country than their own rocks, believe the universe to be an unfinished work, and a scene of unceasing tempest. But the skies do not always lower; the thunder does not incessantly roll, nor the lightnings continually flash; immediately after the most dreadful tempests, the hemisphere clears itself by slow degrees, and becomes serene. The dispositions of the Swiss follow the nature of their climate; kindness succeeds to violence, and generosity to the most brutal fury: this may be easily proved, not only from the records of history, but from recent facts.

General Redin, an inhabitant of the Alps, and a native of the canton of Schwitz, enlisted very early in life into the Swiss Guards, and attained the rank of lieutenant-general in that corps. His long residence at Paris and Versailles, however, had not been able to change his character; he still continued a true Swiss. The new regulation made by the king of France, in the year 1764, relating to this corps, gave great discontent to the canton of Schwitz. The citizens, considering it as an innovation extremely prejudicial to their ancient privileges, threw all the odium of the measures on the lieutenant-general, whose wife, at this period, resided on his estate in the canton, where she endeavored to raise a number of young recruits; but the sound of the French drum had become so disgusting to the ears of the citizens, that they beheld with indignation the white cockade placed in the hats of the deluded peasants. The magistrate apprehensive that this ferment might ultimately cause an insurrection among the people, felt it his duty to forbid madame de Redin to continue her levies. The lady requested he would certify his prohibition in writing; but the magistrate not being disposed to carry matters to this extremity against the court of France, she continued to beat up for the requested number of recruits. The inhabitants of the canton, irritated by this bold defiance of the prohibition, summoned a General Diet, and madame de Redin appeared before the Assembly of Four Thousand. "The drum," said she, "shall never cease to sound, until you give me such a certificate as may justify my husband to the French court for not completing the number of his men." The Assembly accordingly granted her the required certificate, and enjoining her to procure the interest and interposition of her husband with the court in favor of her injured country, waited in anxious expectation that his negotiation would produce a favorable issue. Unhappily the court of Versailles rejected all solicitation on the subject, and by this means drove the irritated and impatient inhabitants beyond the bounds of restraint. The leading men of the canton pretended that the new regulation endangered not only their civil liberties, but, what was dearer to them, their religion. The general discontent was at length fomented into popular fury. A General Diet was again assembled, and it was publicly resolved not to furnish the King of France in future with any troops. The treaty of alliance concluded in the year 1713 was torn from the public register, and general de Redin ordered instantly to return from France with the soldiers under his command, upon pain, if he refused, of being irrevocably banished from the republic. The obedient general obtained permission from the king to depart with his regiment from France, and entering Schwitz, the metropolis of the canton, at the head of his troops, with drums beating and colors flying, marched immediately to the church, where he deposited his standards upon the great altar, and falling on his knees, offered up his thanks to God. Rising from the ground, and turning to his affectionate soldiers, who were dissolved in tears, he discharged their arrears of pay, gave them their uniforms and accoutrements, and bid them forever farewell. The fury of the populace, on perceiving within their power the man whom the whole country considered as the perfidious abettor, and traitorous adviser, of the new regulation, by which the court of Versailles had given such a mortal blow to the liberties of the country, greatly increased; and he was ordered to disclose before the General Assembly the origin of that measure, and the means by which it had been carried on, in order that they might learn their relative situation with France, and ascertain the degree of punishment that was due to the offender. Redin, conscious that, under the existing circumstances, eloquence would make no impression on minds so prejudiced against him, contented himself with coolly declaring, in a few words, that the cause of framing a new regulation was publicly known, and that he was as innocent upon the subject as he was ignorant of the cause of his dismission. "The traitor then will not confess!" exclaimed one of the most furious members: "Hang him on the next tree—cut him to pieces." These menaces were instantly repeated throughout the Assembly; and while the injured soldier continued perfectly tranquil and undismayed, a party of the people, more daring than the rest, jumped upon the tribune, where he stood surrounded by the judges. A young man, his godson, was holding a *parapluie* over his head, to shelter him from the rain, which at this moment poured down in incessant torrents, when one of the enraged multitude immediately broke the *parapluie* in pieces with his stick, exclaiming, "Let the traitor be uncovered!" This exclamation conveyed a correspondent indignation into the bosom of the youth, who instantly replied, "My god-father a betrayer of his country! Oh! I was ignorant, I assure you, of the crime alleged against him; but since it is so, let him perish! Where is the rope? I will be first to put it round the traitor's neck!" The magistrates instantly formed a circle round the general, and with uplifted hands exhorted him to avert the impending danger, by confessing that he had not opposed the measures of France with sufficient zeal, and to offer to the offended people his whole fortune as an atonement for his neglect; representing to him that these were the only means of redeeming his liberty, and perhaps his life. The undaunted soldier, with perfect tranquillity and composure, walked through the surrounding circle to the side of the tribune, and while the whole Assembly anxiously expected to hear an ample confession of his guilt, made a sign of silence with his hand: "Fellow-citizens," said he, "you are not ignorant that I have been two-and-forty years in the French establishment. You know, and many among you, who were with me in the service, can testify its truth, how often I have faced the enemy, and the manner in which I conducted myself in battle. I considered every engagement as the last day of my life. But here I protest to you, in the presence of that Almighty Being who knows all our hearts, who listens to all our words, and who will hereafter judge all our actions, that I never appeared before an enemy with a mind more pure, a conscience more tranquil, a heart more innocent, than at present I possess; and if it is your pleasure to condemn me because I refuse to confess a treachery of which I have not been guilty, I am now ready to resign my life into your hands." The dignified demeanor with which the general made this declaration, and the air of truth which accompanied his words, calmed the fury of the Assembly, and saved his life. Both he and his wife, however, immediately quitted the canton; she entering into a convent at Uri, and he retiring to a cavern among the rocks, where he lived two years in solitude. Time, at length, subdued the anger of the people, and softened the general's sense of their injustice. He returned to the bosom of his country, rewarded its ingratitude by the most signal services, and made every individual recollect and acknowledge the integrity of their magnanimous countryman. To recompense him for the injuries and injustice he had suffered, they elected him bailli, or chief officer of the canton; and afforded him an almost singular instance of their constancy and affection, by successively conferring on him three times this high and important dignity. This is the characteristic disposition of the Swiss who inhabit the Alps; alternately violent and mild: and experiencing, as the extremes of a delighted or vexed imagination happen to prevail, the same vicissitudes as their climate. The rude scenes of greatness which these stupendous mountains and vast deserts afford, render the Swiss violent in sentiment, and rough in manners; while the tranquillity of their fields, and the smiling beauties of their vallies, soften their minds, and render their hearts kind and benevolent.

English artists confess that the aspect of nature in Swisserland is too sublime and majestic for the pencil of art faithfully to reach; but how exquisite must be the enjoyments they feel upon those romantic hills, in those delightful vallies, upon the charming borders of those still and transparent lakes, where nature unfolds her various charms, and appears in the highest pomp and splendor; where the majestic oaks, the deep embowering elms, and dark green firs, which cover and adorn these immense forests, are pleasingly interspersed with myrtles, almond trees, jasmines, pomegranates, and vines, which offer their humbler beauties to the view, and variegate the scene! Nature is in no country of the globe more rich and various than in Swisserland. It was the scenery around Zurich, and the beauties of its adjoining lake, that first inspired the Idylls of the immortal Gessner.

These sublime beauties, while they elevate and inflame the heart, give greater action and life to the imagination than softer scenes; in like manner as a fine night affords a more august and solemn spectacle than the mildest day.

In coming from Frescati, by the borders of the small lake of Nemi, which lies in a deep valley, so closely sheltered by mountains and forest, that the winds are scarcely permitted to disturb its surface, it is impossible not to exclaim with an English poet, that here —

"Black melancholy sits, and round her throws

A death-like silence, and a dread repose:

Her gloomy presence saddens all the scene,

Shades every flower, and darkens every green;

Deepens the murmurs of the falling floods,

And breathes a browner horror on the woods."

But how the soul expands, and every thought becomes serene and free, when, from the garden of the Capuchins, near Albano, the eye suddenly discovers the little melancholy lake, with Frescati and all its rural vallies on one side: on the other, the handsome city of Albano, the village and castle of Riccia and Gensano, with their hills beautifully adorned with clusters of the richest vines: below, the extensive plains of Campania, in the middle of which Rome, formerly the mistress of the world, raises its majestic head; and lastly, beyond all these objects, the hills of Tivoli, the Appenines, and the Mediterranean sea!

How often, on the approach of spring, has the magnificent valley, where the ruins of the residence of Rodolpho de Hapsburg rise upon the side of a hill, crowned with woods of variegated verdure, afforded me the purest and most ineffable delight! There the rapid Aar descends in torrents from the lofty mountains; sometimes forming a vast basin in the vale; at others, precipitating through the narrow passages across the rocks, winding its course majestically through the middle of the vast and fertile plains: on the other side the Ruffs, and, lower down, the Limmat, bring their tributary streams, and peaceably unite them with the waters of the Aar. In the middle of this rich and verdant scene, I beheld the Royal Solitude, where the remains of the emperor Albert I. repose in silence, with those of many princes of the house of Austria, counts, knights, and gentlemen, killed in battle by the gallant Swiss. At a distance I discovered the valley where lie the ruins of the celebrated city of Vindonissa, upon which I have frequently sat, and reflected upon the vanity of human greatness. Beyond this magnificent country, ancient castles raise their lofty heads upon the hills! and the far distant horizon is terminated by the sublime summits of the Alps. In the midst of all this grand scenery, my eyes were instinctively cast down into the deep valley immediately below me, and continually fixed upon the little village where I first drew my breath. It is thus that the sublime or beautiful operates differently on the heart! the one exciting fear and terror, the other creating only soft and agreeable sensations; but both tending to enlarge the sphere of the imagination, and enabling us more completely to seek enjoyment within ourselves.

Pleasures of this description may, indeed be enjoyed, without visiting the romantic solitudes of either Swisserland or Italy. There is no person who may not, while he is quietly traversing the hills and dales, learn to feel how much the aspect of nature may, by the assistance of the imagination, affect the heart. A fine view, the freshness of the air, an unclouded sky, and the joys of the chase, give sensations of health, and make every step seem too short. The privation of all ideas of dependance, accompanied by domestic comfort, useful employments, and innocent recreations, produce a strength of thought, and fertility of imagination, which present to the mind the most agreeable images, and touch the heart with the most delightful sensations. It is certainly true, that a person possessed of a fine imagination may be much happier in prison, than he could possibly be without imagination amidst the most magnificent scenery. But even to a mind deprived of this happy faculty, the lowest enjoyments of rural life, even the common scenery of harvest time, is capable of performing miracles on his heart. Alas! who has not experienced, in the hours of langor and disgust, the powerful effects which a contemplation of the pleasures that surround the poorest peasant's cot is capable of affording! How fondly the heart participates in all his homely joys! With what freedom, cordiality, and kindness, we take him by the hand, and listen to his innocent and artless tales! — How suddenly do we feel an interest in all his little concerns; an interest which, while it unveils, refines and meliorates the latent inclinations of our hearts!

The tranquillity of retired life, and the view of rural scenes, frequently produce a quietude of disposition, which, while it renders the noisy pleasures of the world insipid, enables the heart to seek the charms of solitude with increased delight.

The happy indolence peculiar to Italians, who, under the pleasures of a clear, unclouded sky, are always poor but never miserable, greatly augments the feelings of the heart: the mildness of the climate, the fertility of their soil, their peaceful religion, and their contented nature, compensate for every thing. Dr. Moore, an English traveller, whose works afford me great delight, says, that "the Italians are the greatest loungers in the world; and while walking in the fields, or stretched in the shade, seem to enjoy the serenity and genial warmth of their climate with a degree of luxurious indulgence peculiar to themselves. Without ever running into the daring excesses of the English, or displaying the frisky vivacity of the French, or the stubborn phlegm of the Germans, the Italian populace discover a species of sedate sensibility to every source of enjoyment, from which, perhaps, they derive a greater degree of happiness than any of the others."

Relieved from every afflicting and tormenting object, it is, perhaps, impossible for the mind not to resign itself to agreeable chimeras and romantic sentiments: but this situation notwithstanding these disadvantages, has its fair side. Romantic speculations may lead the mind into certain extravagancies and errors from whence base and contemptible passions may be engendered; may habituate it to a light and frivolous style of thinking; and, by preventing it from directing its faculties to rational ends, may obscure the prospect of true happiness; for the soul cannot easily quit the illusion on which it dwells with such fond delight; the ordinary duties of life, with its more noble and substantial pleasures, are perhaps thereby obstructed: but it is very certain that romantic sentiments do not always render the mind that possesses them unhappy. Who, alas! is so completely happy in reality as he frequently has been in imagination!

Rousseau, who, in the early part of his life, was extremely fond of romances, feeling his mind hurried away by the love of those imaginary objects with which that species of composition abounds, and perceiving the facility with which they may be enjoyed, withdrew his attention from every thing about him, and by this circumstance laid the foundation of that taste for solitude which he preserved to an advanced period of his life; a taste in appearance dictated by depression and disgust, and attributed by him to the irresistible impulse of an affectionate, fond, and tender heart, which, not being able to find in the regions of philosophy and truth sentiments sufficiently warm and animated, was constrained to seek its enjoyments in the sphere of fiction.

But the imagination, may, in retirement, indulge its wanderings to a certain degree without the risk of injuring either the sentiments of the mind or the sensations of the heart. Oh! if the friends of my youth in Swisserland knew how frequently, during the silence of the night, I pass with them those hours which are allotted to sleep; if they were apprized that neither time nor absence can efface the remembrance of their former kindness from my mind, and that this pleasing recollection tends to dissipate my grief, and to cast the veil of oblivion over my woes; they would, perhaps, also rejoice to find that I still live among them in imagination, though I may be dead to them in reality.

The solitary man, whose heart is warmed with refined and noble sentiments, cannot be unhappy.—While the stupid and vulgar bewail his fate, and conceive him to be the victim of corroding care and loathed melancholy, he frequently tastes the most delightful pleasure. The French entertained a notion that Rousseau was a man of a gloomy and dejected disposition; but he was certainly not so for many years of his life, particularly when he wrote to M. de Malesherbes, the chancellor's son, in the following terms: "I cannot express to you, Sir, how sensibly I am affected by perceiving that you think me the most unhappy of mankind; for as the public will, no doubt, entertain the same sentiment of me as you do, it is to me a source of real affliction!— Oh! if my sentiments were really known, every individual would endeavor to follow my example. Peace would then reign throughout the world; men would no longer seek to destroy each other; and wickedness, by removing the great incentives to it, no longer exist. But it may be asked, how I could find employment in solitude?—I answer, in my own mind; in the whole universe; in every thing that dies, in every thing that can exist; in all that the eye finds beautiful in the real, or the imagination in the intellectual world. I assembled about me every thing that is flattering to the heart, and regulated my pleasures by the moderation of my desires. No! The most voluptuous have never experienced such refined delights; and I have always enjoyed my chimeras much more than if they had been realized."

This is certainly the language of enthusiasm; but, ye stupid vulgar! who would not prefer the warm fancy of this amiable philosopher to your cold and creeping understandings?—Who would not willingly renounce your vague conversation, your deceitful felicities, your boasted urbanity, your noisy assemblies, puerile pastimes, and inveterate prejudices, for a quiet and contented life in the bosom of a happy family?—Who would not rather seek in the silence of the woods, or upon the daisied borders of a peaceful lake, those pure and simple pleasures of nature, so delicious in recollection, and productive of joys so pure, so affecting, so different from your own?

Eclogues, which are representatives of rural happiness in its highest perfection, are also fictions; but they are fictions of the most pleasing and agreeable kind. True felicity must be sought in retirement, where the soul, disengaged from the torments of the world, no longer feels those artificial desires which render it unhappy both in prospect and fruition. Content with little, satisfied with all, surrounded by love and innocence, we perceive in retirement, the golden age, as described by the poets, revived; while in the world every one regrets its loss. The regret however, is unjust; for those enjoyments were not peculiar to that happy period; and each individual may, whenever he pleases, form his own Arcadia. The beauties of a crystal spring, a silent grove, a daisied meadow, chasten the feelings of the heart, and afford at all times, to those who have a taste for nature, a permanent and pure delight.

"The origin of poetry," says Pope, "is ascribed to that age which succeeded the creation of the world: as the keeping of flocks seems to have been the first employment of mankind, the most ancient sort of poetry was pastoral. It is natural to imagine, that the leisure of these ancient shepherds admitting and inviting some diversion, none was so proper to that solitary and sedentary life as singing, and that in their songs they took occasion to celebrate their own felicity. From hence a poem was invented, and afterward improved to a perfect image of that happy time, which, by giving us an esteem for the virtues of a former age, might recommend them to the present."

These agreeable though fictitious descriptions of the age of innocence and virtue, communicate joy and gladness to our hearts; and we bless the poet, who, in the ecstacy of his felicity contributes to render others as happy as himself. Sicily and Zurich have produced two of these benefactors to mankind. The aspect of nature never appears more charming, the bosom never heaves with such sweet delight, the heart never beats more pleasantly, the soul never feels more perfect happiness than is produced by reading the Idylls of Theocritus and Gessner.

By these easy simple modes the beauties of nature are made, by the assistance of the imagination, to operate forcibly on the heart. The mind, indeed, drawn away by these agreeable images, often resigns itself too easily to the illusions of romance; but the ideas they create generally amend the heart without injuring the understanding, and spread some of the sweetest flowers along the most thorny paths of human life.

Leisure, the highest happiness upon earth, is seldom enjoyed with perfect satisfaction, except in solitude. Indolence and indifference do not always afford leisure: for true leisure is frequently found in that interval of relaxation which divides a painful duty from the agreeable occupations of literature and philosophy. P. Scipio was of this opinion when he said, that *he was never less idle when he had most leisure,* and that *he was never less alone than when he was alone.* Leisure is not to be considered a state of intellectual torpidity, but a new incentive to further activity; it is sought by strong and energetic minds, not as *an end,* but as *a means* of restoring lost activity; for whoever seeks happiness in a situation merely quiescent, seeks for a phantom that will elude his grasp. Leisure will never be found in mere rest; but will follow those who seize the first impulse to activity; in which, however, such employments as best suit the extent and nature of different capacities, must be preferred to those which promise compensation without labor, and enjoyment without pain.

Thus rural retirement dries up those streams of discontent which flow so plentifully through public life; changes most frequently the bitterest feeling into the sweetest pleasures; and inspires an ecstacy and content unknown to the votaries of the world. The tranquillity of nature buries in oblivion the criminal inclinations of the heart; renders it blithe, tender, open, and confident; and, by wisely managing the passions, and preventing an overheated imagination from fabricating fancied woes, strengthens in it every virtuous sensation.

In towns, the solitude which is necessary to produce this advantage cannot be conveniently practised. It seems indeed, no very difficult task for a man to retire into his chamber, and by silent contemplation, to raise his mind above the mean consideration of sensual objects; but few men have sufficient resolution to perform it; for, within doors, matters of business every moment occur, and interrupt the chain of reflection; and without, whether alone or in company, a variety of accidents may occasionally happen, which will confound our vain wisdom, aggravate the painful feelings of the heart, and weaken the finer powers of the mind.

Rousseau was always miserable during his residence at Paris. This extraordinary genius, it is true, wrote his immortal works in that agitated metropolis; but the moment he quitted his study, and wandered through the streets, his mind was bewildered by a variety of heterogeneous sentiments, his recollection vanished; and this brilliant writer and profound philosopher, who was so intimately acquainted with the most intricate labyrinths of the human heart, was reduced to the condition of a child. But in the country we issue from the house in perfect safety, and feel increasing cheerfulness and satisfaction. Tired with meditation, the rural recluse has only to open the doors of his study, and enjoy his walk, while tranquillity attends his steps, and new pleasures present themselves to his view on every turn. Beloved by all around him, he extends his hand with cordial affection to every man he meets. Nothing occurs to vex and irritate his mind. He runs no risk of being tortured by the supercilious behavior of some haughty female proud of her descent, or of enduring the arrogant egotism of an upstart peer: is in no danger of being crushed beneath the rolling carriages of Indian nabobs: nor dares frontless vice, on the authority of mouldy parchments, attack his property, or presumptuous ignorance offer the least indignity to his modest virtue.

A man, indeed, by avoiding the tumultuous intercourse of society, and deriving his comforts from his own breast, may, even in Paris, or any other metropolis, avoid these unpleasant apprehensions, if his nerves be firm, and his constitution strong: for to a frame disjointed by nervous affections every object is irritating, and every passion tremblingly alive. The passions are the gales by which man must steer his course through the troubled ocean of life; they fill the sails which give motion to the soul; and when they become turbulent and impetuous, the vessel is always in danger, and generally runs aground. The petty cares and trifling vexations of life, however, give but shortlived disturbance to a heart free from remorse. Philosophy teaches us to forget past uneasiness, to forbear idle speculations of approaching felicity, and to rest contented with present comforts, without refining away our existing happiness by wishing that which is really good to be still better. Every thing is much better than we imagine. A mind too anxious in the expectation of happiness is seldom satisfied, and generally mixes with its highest fruition a certain portion of discontent. The stream of content must flow from a deliberate disposition in our minds to learn what is good, and a determined resolution to seek for and enjoy it, however small the portion may be.

The content, however, which men in general so confidently expect to find in rural retirement, is not to be acquired by viewing objects either with indiscriminate admiration or supine indifference. He who without labor, and without a system of conduct previously digested and arranged, hopes for happiness in solitude, will yawn with equal fatigue at his cottage in the country and his mansion in town; while he who keeps himself continually employed, may in the deepest solitude, by the mere dint of labor, attain true tranquillity and happiness.

Petrarch, in his solitude at Vaucluse, would have experienced this tranquillity, if his bosom had not been disturbed by love; for he perfectly understood the art of managing his time. "I rise," said he, "before the sun, and on the approach of day wander contemplatively along the fields, or retire to study. I read, I write, I think, I vanquish indolence, banish sleep, avoid luxury, and forget sensuality. From morning till night I climb the barren mountains, traverse the humid vallies, seek the deepest caves, or walk, accompanied only by my thoughts, along the banks of my river. I have no society to distract my mind; and men daily become less annoying to me; for I place them either far before or far behind me. I recollect what is past, and contemplate on what is to come. I have found an excellent expedient to detach my mind from the world. I cultivate a fondness for my place of residence, and I am persuaded that I could be happy any where except at Avignon. In my retreat at Vaucluse, where I am at present, I occasionally find Athens, Rome, or Florence, as the one or the other of those places happens to please the prevailing disposition of my mind. Here I enjoy all my friends, as well as those who have long since entered the vale of death, and of whom I have no knowledge, but what their works afford."

What character, however luxurious, ever felt the same content at any splendid entertainment, as Rousseau experienced in his humble meal! "I return home," says he, "with tired feet, but with a contented mind, and experience the calmest repose in resigning myself to the impression of objects, without exercising thought, indulging imagination, or doing any thing to interrupt the peaceful felicity of my station. The table is ready spread on my lawn, and furnished with refreshments. Surrounded by my small and happy family, I eat my supper with healthy appetite, and without any appearance of servitude or dependance to annoy the love and kindness by which we are united. My faithful dog is not a subservient slave, but a firm friend, from whom, as we always feel the same inclination, I never exact obedience. The gaiety of the mind throughout the evening testifies that I live alone throughout the day; for, being seldom pleased with others, and never, when visiters have disturbed me, with myself, I sit, during the whole evening of the day when company has interrupted me, either grumbling or in silence: so at least my good housekeeper has remarked; and since she mentioned it, I have from my own observation found it universally true. Having thus made my humble and cheerful meal, I take a few turns round my little garden, or play some favorite air upon my spinette, and experience upon my pillow a soft content, more sweet, if possible, than even undisturbed repose."

At the village of Richterswyl, situated a few leagues from Zurich, and surrounded by every object the most smiling, beautiful, and romantic that Swisserland presents, dwells a celebrated physician. His soul, like the scenery of nature which surrounds him, is tranquil and sublime. His habitation is the temple of health, of friendship, and of every peaceful virtue. The village rises on the borders of the lake, at a place where two projecting points form a fine bay of nearly half a league. On the opposite shores, the lake, which is not quite a league in extent, is enclosed from the north to the east by pleasant hills covered with vineyards, intermixed with fertile meadows, orchards, fields, groves, and thickets, with little hamlets, churches, villas, and cottages scattered up and down the scene. A wide and magnificent amphitheatre, which no artist has yet attempted to paint, except in detached scenes, opens itself from the east to the south. The view towards the higher part of the lake, which on this side is four leagues long, presents to the eye jutting points of land, detached aytes, the little town of Rapperschwyl, built on the side of a hill, and a bridge which reaches from one side of the lake to the other. Beyond the town the inexhaustible valley extends itself in a half circle to the sight; and upon the foreground rises a peak of land which swells as it extends into beautiful hills. Behind them, at the distance of about half a league, is a range of mountains covered with trees and verdure, and interspersed with villages and detached houses; beyond which, at a still greater distance, are discovered the fertile and majestic Alps, twisted one among the other, and exhibiting, alternately, shades of the lightest and darkest azure: and in the back ground high rocks, covered with eternal snows, lift their towering heads, and touch the skies. On the south side of this rich, enchanting, and incomparable scene, the amphitheatre is extended by another range of mountains reaching toward the west; and at the feet of these mountains, on the borders of the lake, lies the village of Richterswyl, surrounded by rich fallows and fertile pastures, and overhung by forests of firs. The streets of the village, which in itself is extremely clean, are nearly paved; and the houses, which are mostly built of stone, are painted on the outside. Pleasant walks are formed along the banks of the lake, and lead quite round the town, through groves of fruit-trees and shady forests, up to the very summit of the hills. The traveller, struck with the sublime and beautiful scenery that every where surrounds him, stops to contemplate with eager curiosity the increasing beauties which ravish his sight; and while his bosom swells with excess of pleasure, his suspended breath bespeaks his fear of interrupting the fulness of his delight. Every acre of this charming country is in the highest state of cultivation and improvement. Every hand is at work; and men, women, and children, of every age and of every description, are all usefully employed.

The two houses of the physician are each of them surrounded by a garden; and although situated in the centre of the village, are as rurally sequestered as if they had been built in the bosom of the country. Through the gardens, and close beneath the chamber of my valued friend, runs a pure and limpid stream, on the opposite of which, at an agreeable distance, is the high road; where, almost daily, numbers of pilgrims successively pass in their way to the hermitage. From the windows of these houses, and from every part of the gardens, you behold, toward the south, at the distance of about a league, the majestic Ezelberg rear its lofty head, which is concealed in forests of deep green firs; while on its declivity hangs a neat little village, with a handsome church, upon the steeple of which the sun suspends his departing rays, and shows its career is nearly finished. In the front is the lake of Zurich, whose peaceful water is secured from the violence of tempests, and whose transparent surface reflects the beauties of its delightful banks.

During the silence of the night, if you repair to the chamber windows of this enchanting mansion, or walk through its gardens, to taste the exhaling fragrance of the shrubs and flowers, while the moon, rising in unclouded majesty over the summit of the mountains, reflects on the smooth surface of the water a broad beam of light, you hear, during this awful sleep of nature, the sound of the village clocks, echoing from the opposite shores; and, on the Richterswyl side, the shrill proclamation of the watchmen, blended occasionally with the barkings of the faithful house-dog. At a distance you hear the boats gliding gently along the stream, dividing the water with their oars, and perceive them, as they cross the moon's translucent beam, playing among the sparkling waves.

Riches and luxury are no where to be seen in the happy habitation of this wise philanthropist. His chairs are made of straw; his tables are worked from the wood of the country; and the plates and dishes on which he entertains his friends are all of earthen-ware. Neatness and convenience reign throughout. Drawings, paintings, and engravings, of which he has a large well-chosen collection, are his sole expense. The earliest beams of Aurora light the humble apartment where this philosophic sage sleeps in undisturbed repose, and awake him to new enjoyments every day. As he rises from his bed, the cooing of the turtle-doves, and the morning songs of various kinds of birds, who make their nightly nests in an adjoining aviary, salute his ears, and welcome his approach. The first hour of the morning, and the last at night, are sacred to himself; but he devotes all the intermediate hours of every day to a sick and afflicted multitude, who daily attend him for advice and assistance. The benevolent exercise of his professional skill, indeed, engrosses almost every moment of his life, but it constitutes his highest happiness and joy. The inhabitants of the mountains of Swisserland, and of the vallies of the Alps, flock to his house, and endeavor in vain to find language capable of expressing to him the grateful feelings of their hearts for the favors they receive from him. Convinced of his affection, satisfied of his medical skill, and believing that the good doctor is equally well acquainted with every subject, they listen with the deepest attention to his words, answer all his inquiries without the least hesitation or reserve, treasure up his advice and counsel with more solicitude than if they were grains of gold, and depart from his presence with more regret, comfort, hope, resignation, and virtuous feelings, than if they had quitted their confessor at the hermitage. It may perhaps be conceived, that after a day spent in this manner, the happiness which this friend to mankind must feel cannot in any degree be increased. But, when a simple, innocent, and ingenuous country girl, whose mind has been almost distracted by the fear of losing her beloved husband, enters his study, and seizing him with transport by the hand, joyfully exclaims, "Oh! Sir, my dear husband, ill as he was only two days since, is now quite recovered! Oh! my dear Sir, how, how shall I thank you!" this philanthropic character feels that transcending felicity, which ought to fill the bosom of a monarch in rendering happiness to his people.

Of this description is the country of Swisserland, where doctor Hotze, the ablest physician of the present age, resides; a physician and philosopher, whose variety of knowledge, profound judgment, and great experience, have raised him to an equal eminence with Trissot and Hirtzel, the dearest friends of my heart. It is in this manner that he passes the hours of his life, with uniformity and happiness. Surrounded, except during the two hours I have already mentioned, by a crowd of unfortunate fellow-creatures, who look up to him for relief, his mind, active and full of vigor, never knows repose; but his labors are richly rewarded by the high and refined felicity which fills his heart. Palaces, alas! seldom contain such characters. Individuals, however, of every description may cultivate and enjoy an equal degree of felicity, although they do not reside among scenes so delightful as those which surround my beloved Hotze at Richterswyl, as those of the convent of Capuchins near Albano, or as those which surround the rural retreat of my sovereign George III. at Windsor.

Content can only be found in the tranquillity of the heart; and in solitude the bosom gladly opens to receive the wished-for inmate, and to welcome its attendant virtues. While nature smiles around us, decorated in all its beauties, the heart expands to the cheering scene; every object appears in the most favorable and pleasing point of view; our souls overflow with kind affections; the antipathies created by the ingratitude of the world instantly vanish; we even forget the vain, the wicked, the profligate characters with whom we were mixed; and being perfectly at peace with ourselves, we feel ourselves at peace with all mankind. But in society the rancorous contention which jarring interests daily create, the heavy yoke which subordination is continually imposing, "the oppressor's wrong, the proud man's contumely," and the shocks which reason and good sense hourly receive from fools in power, and insolent superiors, spread torrents of misery over human life, embitter the happiness of their more worthy though inferior fellow-creatures, poison all pleasure, break through social order, spread thorns in the paths of virtue, and render the world a vale of tears.

Blockheads in power are of all other characters, the most baneful and injurious; they confound all just distinctions, mistake one quality for another; degrade every person and thing to their own level; and in short, change white into black, and black into white. To escape from the persecution of such characters, men even of fine talents and ingenious dispositions must act like the fox of Saadi, of the Persian poet. A person one day observing a fox running with uncommon speed to earth, called out to him, "Reynard, where are you running in so great a hurry! Have you been doing any mischief, for which you are apprehensive of punishment?" — "No, Sir," replied the fox, "my conscience is perfectly clear, and does not reproach me with any thing; but I have just overheard the hunters wish that they had *a camel* to hunt this morning." — "Well, but how does that concern you? you are not *a camel*." — "Oh, my good Sir," replied the fox, "are you not aware that sagacious heads have always enemies at their heels? and if any one should point me out to those sportsmen, and cry, *there runs a camel*, they would immediately seize me without examining whether I was really the kind of animal the informer had described me to be." Reynard was certainly right in his conclusion; for men are in general wicked in proportion as they are ignorant or envious, and the only means of eluding their mischievous intentions is to keep out of their way.

The simplicity, regularity, and serenity which accompany retirement, moderate the warmest tempers, guard the heart against the intrusion of inordinate desires, and at length render it invulnerable to the shafts of malice and detraction; while the self-examination it necessarily imposes, teaches us, by exhibiting to our view our own defects, to do justice to the superior merit of others. The delightful solitudes of Lausanne exhibit every where captivating examples of domestic felicity. The industrious citizen, after having faithfully performed his daily task, is sure of experiencing, on his return at evening to his wife and children, real comfort and unalloyed content. The voice of slander, the neglect of ingratitude, the contempt of superiors, and all the mortifications attendant upon worldly intercourse, are forgot the moment he beholds his happy family ready with open arms to receive him, and to bestow upon their friend and benefactor the fond caresses he so justly merits. With what exquisite delight his beating bosom feels their rapturous affection. If his mind has been vexed by the crosses of life, the ostentation of courts, the insolence of riches, the arrogance of power, or his temper irritated and soured by the base practices of fraud, falsehood, or hypocrisy, he no sooner mixes with those whom he cherishes and supports, than a genial warmth reanimates his dejected heart, the tenderest sentiments inspire his soul, and the truth, the freedom, the probity, and the innocence by which he is surrounded, tranquillize his mind, and reconcile him to his humble lot. Oh! observe him, all ye who are placed in more elevated stations, whether ye enjoy the confidence of statesmen, are the beloved companions of the great, the admired favorites of the fair, the envied leaders of the public taste, of high birth, or of ample fortunes; for if your rich and splendid homes be the seats of jealousy and discord, and the bosoms of your families strangers to that content which the wise and virtuous feel within walls of clay, and under roofs of humble thatch, you are, in comparison, poor indeed.

Characters enervated by prosperity feel the smallest inconvenience as a serious calamity, and, unable to bear the touch of rude and violent hands, require to be treated, like young and tender flowers, with delicacy, and attention; while those who have been educated in the rough school of adversity, walk over the thorns of life with a firm and intrepid step, and kick them from the path with indifference and contempt. Superior to the false opinions and prejudices of the world, they bear with patient fortitude the blow of misfortune, disregard all trifling injuries, and look down with proud contempt on the malice of their enemies, and the infidelity of their friends.

The lofty zephyr, the transparent spring, the well-stored river, the umbrageous forest, the cooling grotto, and the daisied field, however, are not always necessary to enable us to despise or forget the consequences of adversity. The man who firmly keeps his course, and has courage to live according to his own taste and inclinations, cannot be affected by the little crosses of life, or by the obloquy or injustice of mankind. What we do voluntarily always affords us more pleasure than that which we do by compulsion. The restraints of the world and the obligations of society, disgust liberal minds, and deprive them, even in the midst of all their splendor and fortune, of that content they seek so anxiously to obtain.

Solitude, indeed, not only tranquillizes the heart, renders it kind and virtuous, and raises it above the malevolence of envy, wickedness, and conceited ignorance, but affords advantages still more valuable. Liberty, true liberty, flies from the tumultuous crowd, and the forced connexions of the world. It has been truly observed, that in solitude man recovers from the distraction which had torn him from himself; feels a clear conception of what he once was, and may yet become; explores the nature, and discovers the extent, of his freeborn character: rejects every thing artificial; is guided by his own sentiments; no longer dreads a severe master or imperious tyrant; and neither suffers the constraints of business or the blandishments of pleasure, to disturb his repose; but, breaking boldly through the shackles of servile habit and arbitrary custom, thinks for himself with confidence and courage, and improves the sensibility of his heart by the sentiments of his mind.

Madame de Stael considered it a great error, to imagine that freedom and liberty could be indulged at court, where the mind, even on the most trifling occasions, is obliged to observe a multitude of ceremonies, where it is impossible to speak one's thoughts, where our sentiments must be adapted to those around us, where every person assumes a control over us, and where we never have the smallest enjoyment of ourselves. "To enjoy ourselves," says she, "we must seek solitude. It was in the Bastile that I first became acquainted with myself."

A courtier, fearful of every person around him, is continually upon the watch, and tormented incessantly by suspicion; but while his heart is thus a prey to corroding anxiety, he is obliged to appear contented and serene, and, like the old lady, is always lighting one taper to Michael the archangel, and another to the devil, because he does not know for which of them he may have most occasion. A man of a liberal, enlightened mind, is as little calculated to perform the office of master of the ceremonies, or to conduct the etiquette of a court, as a woman is to be *a religieuse.*

Liberty and leisure render a rational and active mind indifferent to every other kind of happiness. It was the love of liberty and solitude which rendered the riches and honors of the world so odious to Petrarch. Solicited at an advanced period of his life, to act as secretary to several popes, under the tempting offer of great emolument, he replied, "Riches when acquired at the expense of liberty, become the source of real misery. A yoke formed of gold and silver is not less galling and restrictive than one made of wood or iron." And he frankly told his friends and patrons, that to him there was no quantity of wealth equal in value to his ease and liberty: that, as he had despised riches at a time when he was most in need of them, it would be shameful in him to seek them now, when he could more conveniently live without them: that every man ought to apportion the provision for his journey according to the distance he had to travel; and that, having almost reached the end of his course, he ought to think more of his *reception at the inn,* than of his *expenses on the road.*

Petrarch, disgusted by the vicious manners which surrounded the papal chair, retired into solitude when he was only three-and-twenty years of age, and in possession of that exterior, both with respect to person and dress, which forms so essential a part in the character of an accomplished courtier. Nature had decorated him with every pleasing attribute. His fine form struck observers so forcibly, that they stopped as he passed along to admire and point out his symmetry. His eyes were bright and full of fire; his lively countenance proclaimed the vivacity of the mind; the freshest color glowed on his cheeks; his features were uncommonly expressive; and his whole appearance was manly, elegant, and noble. The natural disposition of his heart, increased by the warm climate of Italy, the fire of youth, the seductive charms of the various beauties who resorted to the papal court, from every nation of Europe, and especially the prevailing dissipation of the age, attached him, very early in life, to the society of women. The decoration of dress deeply engaged his attention; and the least spot or improper fold on his garments, which were always of the lightest color, seemed to give him real uneasiness. Every form which appeared inelegant was carefully avoided, even in the fashion of his shoes; which were so extremely tight, and cramped him to such a degree, that he would soon have been deprived of the use of his feet, if he had not wisely recollected, that it was much better to displease the eyes of the ladies than to make himself a cripple. To prevent the dress of his hair from being discomposed, he protected it with anxiety from the rudeness of the winds as he passed along the streets. Devoted, however, as he was to the service of the sex, he maintained a rival fondness for literature, and an inviolable attachment to moral sentiment; and while he celebrated the charms of his fair favorites in choice Italian, he reserved his knowledge of the learned languages for subjects more serious and important. Nor did he permit the warmth of his constitution, or the sensibility of his heart, great and exquisite as they were, to debauch his mind, or betray him into the most trifling indiscretion, without feeling the keenest compunction and repentance. "I wish," said he, "that I had a heart as hard as adamant, rather than be so continually tormented by such seducing passions." The heart of this amiable young man, was, indeed, continually assailed by the crowd of beauties that adorned the papal court; and the power of their charms, and the facility with which his situation enabled them to enjoy his company, rendered him in some degree their captive; but, alarmed by the approaching torments and disquietudes of love, he cautiously avoided their pleasing snares, and continued, previous to the sight of his beloved Laura, to roam "free and unconquered through the wilds of love."

The practice of the civil law was at this period the only road to eminence at Avignon; but Petrarch detested the venality of the profession; and though he practised at the bar, and gained many causes by his eloquence, he afterwards reproached himself with it. "In my youth," says he, "I devoted myself to the trade of selling words, or rather fabricating falsehoods; but that which we do against our own inclinations, is seldom attended with success; my fondness was for solitude, and therefore I attended the practice of the bar with aversion and disgust." The secret consciousness however, which he entertained of his own merit, gave him all the confidence natural to youth; and, filling his mind with that lofty spirit which begets the presumption of being equal to the highest achievements, he relinquished the *bar* for the *church*; but his inveterate hatred of the manners of the Episcopal court prevented his exertions, and retarded his promotion. "I have no hope," said he, in the thirty-fifth year of his age, "of making my fortune in the court of the vicar of Jesus Christ; to accomplish that, I must assiduously attend the palaces of the great, and practise flattery, falsehood, and deceit." A task of this kind was too painful to his feelings to perform; not because he either hated the society of men, or disliked advancement, but because he detested the means he must necessarily have used to gratify his ambition. Glory was his warmest wish, and he ardently endeavored to obtain it; not, indeed, by the ways in which it is usually obtained, but by delighting to walk in the most unfrequented paths, and of course, by retiring from the world. The sacrifices he made to solitude were great and important; but his mind and his heart were formed to enjoy the advantages it affords with a superior degree of delight; a happiness which resulted to him from his hatred of a profligate court, and from his love of liberty.

The love of liberty was the secret cause which gave the mind of Rousseau so inveterate a disgust to society, and became in solitude the spring of all his pleasures. His Letters to Malesherbes are as remarkable for the discovery they make of his real disposition, as his Confessions, which have been as much misunderstood as his character. "I mistook for a great length of time," says he, in one of these letters, "the cause of that invincible disgust which I always felt in my intercourse with the world. I attributed it to the mortification of not possessing that quick and ready talent necessary to display in conversation the little knowledge I possessed; and this reflected an idea, that I did not hold that reputation in the opinion of mankind which I conceived I merited. But although, after scribbling many ridiculous things, and perceiving myself sought after by all the world, and honored with much more consideration than even my own ridiculous vanity would have led me to expect, I found that I was in no danger of being taken for a fool; yet, still feeling the same disgust rather augmented than diminished, I concluded that it must arise from some other cause, and that these were not the kind of enjoyments which I must look for. What then, in fact, was the cause of it? It was no other than that invincible spirit of liberty which nothing can overcome, and in competition with which, honor, fortune, and even fame itself, are to me as nothing. It is certain that this spirit of liberty is engendered less by pride than by indolence; but this indolence is incredible; it is alarmed at every thing; it renders the most trifling duties of civil life insupportable. To be obliged to speak a word, to write a letter, or to pay a visit, are to me, from the moment the obligation arises, the severest punishments. This is the reason why, although the ordinary commerce of men is odious to me, the pleasures of private friendship are so dear to my heart; for in the indulgence of private friendships there are no duties to perform; we have only to follow the feelings of the heart, and all is done. This is the reason also why I have so much dreaded to accept of favors; for every act of kindness demands an acknowledgment, and I feel that my heart is ungrateful only because gratitude becomes a duty. The kind of happiness, in short, which pleases me best, does not consist so much in doing what I wish, as in avoiding that which is disagreeable to me. Active life affords no temptations to me. I would much rather do nothing at all than that which I dislike; and I have frequently thought that I should not have lived very unhappily even in the Bastile, provided I was free from any other constraint than that of merely residing within the walls."

An English author asks, "Why are the inhabitants of the rich plains of Lombardy, where nature pours her gifts in such profusion, less opulent than those of the mountains of Swisserland?—Because freedom, whose influence is more benign than sunshine and zephyrs; who covers the rugged rock with soil, drains the sickly swamp, and clothes the brown heath in verdure; who dresses the laborer's face with smiles, and makes him behold his increasing family with delight and exultation—Freedom has abandoned the fertile fields of Lombardy, and dwells among the mountains of Swisserland." This observation, though dressed in such enthusiastic expressions, is literally true at Uri, Schwitz, Underwalde, Zug, Glaris, and Appenzel; for those who have more than their wants require are *rich*; and those who are enabled to think, to speak, and to act as inclination may dictate, are *free*.

Competency and liberty, therefore, are the true sweeteners of life. That state of mind, so rarely possessed, in which a man can sincerely say, *I have enough*, is the highest attainment of philosophy. Happiness does not consist in having much, but in having sufficient. This is the reason why kings and princes are seldom happy; for they always desire more than they possess, and are urged incessantly to attempt more than it is in their power to achieve. He who wants little has always enough. "I am contented," says Petrarch, in a letter to his friends, the cardinals Talleyrand and Bologna: "I desire nothing more; I enjoy every thing that is necessary to life. Cincinnatus, Curtius, Fabricius, and Regulus, after having conquered nations, and led kings in triumph, were not so rich as I am. But I should always be poor if I were to open a door to my passions. Luxury, ambition, avarice know no bounds, and desire is an unfathomable abyss. I have clothes to cover me; victuals to support me; horses to carry me; lands to lie down or walk upon while I live, and to receive my remains when I die. What more was any Roman emperor possessed of?—My body is healthy; and being engaged in toil, is less rebellious against my mind. I have books of every kind, which are to me inestimable treasures; they fill my soul with a voluptuous delight, untinctured with remorse. I have friends whom I consider more precious than any thing I possess, provided their counsels do not tend to abridge my liberty: and I know of no other enemies than those which envy has raised against me."

Solitude not only restrains inordinate desires, but discovers to mankind their real wants; and where a simplicity of manners prevails, the real wants of men are not only few, but easily satisfied; for being ignorant of those desires which luxury creates, they can have no idea of indulging them. An old country curate, who had all his life resided upon a lofty mountain near the lake of Thun, in the canton of Berne, was one day presented with a moor-cock. The good old man, ignorant that such a bird existed, consulted with his cook-maid in what manner this rarity was to be disposed of, and they both agreed to bury it in the garden. If we were all, alas! as ignorant of the delicious flavor of moor-cocks, we might be all as happy and contented as the simple pastor of the mountain near the lake of Thun.

The man who confines his desires to his real wants, is more wise, more rich, and more contented, than any other mortal existing. The system upon which he acts is, like his soul, replete with simplicity and true greatness; and seeking his felicity in innocent obscurity and peaceful retirement, he devotes his mind to the love of truth, and finds his highest happiness in a contented heart.

A calm and tranquil life renders the indulgence of sensual pleasures less dangerous. The theatre of sensuality exhibits scenes of waste and brutality, of noisy mirth and tumultuous riot; presents to observation pernicious goblets, overloaded tables, lascivious dancing, receptacles for disease, tombs with faded roses, and all the dismal haunts of pain. But to him who retires in detestation from such gross delights, the joys of sense are of a more elevated kind; soft, sublime, pure, permanent, and tranquil.

Petrarch one day inviting his friend, the cardinal Colonna, to visit his retirement at Vaucluse, wrote to him, "If you prefer the tranquillity of the country to the noise of the town, come here and enjoy yourself. Do not be alarmed by the simplicity of my table, or the hardness of my beds. Kings themselves are frequently disgusted by the luxury in which they live, and sigh for comforts of a more homely kind. Change of scene is always pleasing; and pleasures, by occasional interruption, frequently become more lively. If, however, you should not accord with these sentiments you may bring with you the most exquisite viands, the wines of Vesuvius, silver dishes, and every thing else that the indulgence of your senses requires. Leave the rest to me. I promise to provide you with a bed of the finest turf, a cooling shade, the music of the nightingales, figs, raisins, water drawn from the freshest springs; and, in short, every thing that the hand of Nature prepares for the lap of genuine pleasure."

Ah! who would not willingly renounce those things which only produce disquietude in the mind, for those which render it contented! The art of occasionally diverting the imagination, taste, and passions, affords new and unknown enjoyments to the mind and confers pleasure without pain, and luxury without repentance. The senses deadened by satiety, revive to new enjoyments. The lively twitter of the groves, and the murmur of the brooks, yield a more delicious pleasure to the ear than the music of the opera, or the compositions of the ablest masters. The eye reposes more agreeably on the concave firmament, on an expanse of waters, on mountains covered with rocks, than it does on all the glare of balls and assemblies. In short, the mind enjoys in solitude objects which were before insupportable, and reclining on the bosom of simplicity, easily renounces every vain delight. Petrarch wrote from Vaucluse to one of his friends, "I have made war against my corporeal powers, for I find they are my enemies. My eyes, which have rendered me guilty of so many follies, are now confined to the view of a single woman, old, black, and sunburnt. If Helen, or Lucretia had possessed such a face, Troy would never have been reduced to ashes, nor Tarquin driven from the empire of the world. But, to compensate these defects, she is faithful, submissive, and industrious. She passes whole days in the fields, her shrivelled skin defying the hottest rays of the sun. My wardrobe still contains fine clothes, but I never wear them; and you would take me for a common laborer or a simple shepherd; I, who formerly was so anxious about my dress. But the reasons which then prevailed, no longer exist: the fetters by which I was enslaved are broken: the eyes which I was anxious to please are shut; and if they were still open, they would not perhaps, now be able to maintain the same empire over my heart."

Solitude, by stripping worldly objects of the false splendor in which fancy arrays them, dispels all vain ambition from the mind. Accustomed to rural delights and indifferent to every other kind of pleasure, a wise man no longer thinks high offices and worldly advancement worthy of his desires. A noble Roman was overwhelmed with tears on being obliged to accept of the consulship, because it would deprive him for one year of the opportunity of cultivating his fields. Cincinnatus, who was called from the plough to the supreme command of the Roman legions, defeated the enemies of his country, added to it new provinces, made his triumphal entry into Rome, and at the expiration of sixteen days returned to his plough. It is true, that the inmate of an humble cottage, who is forced to earn his daily bread by labor, and the owner of a spacious mansion, for whom every luxury is provided, are not held in equal estimation by mankind. But let the man who has experienced both these situations, be asked under which of them he felt the most content. The cares and inquietudes of the palace are innumerably greater than those of the cottage. In the former, discontent poisons every enjoyment; and its superfluity is only misery in disguise. The princes of Germany do not digest all the palatable poison which their cooks prepare, so well as a peasant upon the heaths of Limbourg digests his buck-wheat pie. And those who may differ from me in this opinion, will be forced to acknowledge, that there is great truth in the reply which a pretty French country girl, made to a young nobleman, who solicited her to abandon her rustic taste, and retire with him to Paris: "Ah! my lord, the further we remove from ourselves, the greater is our distance from happiness."

Solitude, by moderating the selfish desires of the heart, and expelling ambition from the breast, becomes a real asylum to the disappointed statesman or discarded minister; for it is not every public minister who can retire, like Neckar, through the portals of everlasting fame. Every person, indeed, without distinction, ought to raise his grateful hands to heaven, on being dismissed from the troubles of public life, to the calm repose which the cultivation of his native fields, and the care of his flocks and herds, afford. In France, however, when a minister, who has incurred the displeasure of his sovereign, is ordered to *retire*, and thereby enabled to visit an estate which he has decorated in the highest style of rural elegance, this delightful retreat, alas! being considered a place of exile, becomes intolerable to his mind: he no longer fancies himself its master; is incapable of relishing its enchanting beauties; repose flies from his pillow; and turning with aversion from every object, he dies at length, the victim of spleen, petulance, and dejection. But in England it is just the reverse. There a minister is congratulated on retiring, like a man who has happily escaped from a dangerous malady. He feels himself still surrounded by many friends much more worthy than his adherents while in power; for while those were bound to him by temporary considerations of interest, these are attached to him by real and permanent esteem. Thanks, generous Britons! for the examples you have given to us of men sufficiently bold and independent to weigh events in the scales of reason, and to guide themselves by the intrinsic and real merits of each case: for notwithstanding the freedom with which many Englishmen have arraigned the dispensations of the Supreme Being; notwithstanding the mockery and ridicule with which they have so frequently insulted virtue, good manners, and decorum; there are many more among them, who, especially at an advanced period of their lives, perfectly understand the art of living by themselves; and in their tranquil and delightful villas think with more dignity, and live with more real happiness, than the haughtiest noble in the zenith of his power.

Of the ministers who retire from the administration of public affairs, the majority finish their days in cultivating their gardens, in improving their estates, and, like the excellent de la Roche, at Spire, certainly possess more content with the shovel and the rake, than they enjoyed in the most prosperous hours in their administration.

It has, indeed, been said, that observations like these are common to persons who, ignorant of the manners of the world, and the characters of men, love to moralize on, and recommend a contempt of, human greatness; but that rural innocence, the pure and simple pleasures of nature, and an uninterrupted repose, are very seldom the companions of this boasted solitude. Those who maintain this opinion, assert, that man, though surrounded with difficulties, and obliged to employ every art and cunning to attain his ends, feels with his success the pleasing power which attaches to the character of master, and fondly indulges in the exercise of sovereignty. Enabled to create and to destroy, to plant and to root up, to make alterations when and where he pleases, he may grub up a vineyard, and plant an English grove on its site; erect hills where hills never were seen; level eminences to the ground; compel the stream to flow as his inclination shall direct; force woods and shrubberies to grow where he pleases; graft or lop as it shall strike his fancy; open views and shut out boundaries; construct ruins where buildings never existed; erect temples of which he alone is the high priest; and build hermitages in which he may seclude himself at pleasure. It is said, however, that this is not a reward for the restraints he formerly experienced, but a natural inclination; for that a minister must be, from the habits of his life, fond of command and sovereignty, whether he continues at the head of an extensive empire, or directs the management of a poultry yard.

It would most undoubtedly discover a great ignorance of the world, and of the nature of man, to contend that it is necessary to renounce all the inclinations of the human heart, in order to enjoy the advantages of solitude. That which nature has implanted in the human breast must there remain. If, therefore a minister, in his retirement, is not satiated with the exercise of power and authority, but still fondly wishes for command, let him require obedience from his chickens, provided such a gratification is essential to his happiness and tends to suppress the desire of again exposing himself to those tempests and shipwrecks which he can only avoid in the safe harbor of rural life. An ex-minister must sooner or later, learn to despise the appearances of human greatness, when he discovers that true greatness frequently begins at that period of life which statesmen are apt to consider a dreary void; that the regret of being no longer able to do more good, is only ambition in disguise; and that the inhabitants of the country, in cultivating their cabbages and potatoes, are a hundred times happier than the greatest minister.

Nothing contributes more to the advancement of earthly felicity, than a reliance on those maxims which teach us to *do as much good as possible*, and *to take things just as we find them*; for it is certainly true that no characters are so unhappy as those who are continually finding fault with every thing they see. My barber at Hanover, while he was preparing to shave me, exclaimed, with a deep sigh, "*It is terribly hot to day,*" "You place heaven," said I to him, "in great difficulties. For these nine months last past, you have regularly told me every other day, *It is terribly cold to day.*" Cannot the Almighty, then any longer govern the universe, without these gentlemen barbers finding something to be discontented with? "Is it not," I asked him, "much better to take the seasons as they change, and to receive with equal gratitude, from the hand of God, the winter's cold, and the summer's warmth?" "Oh! certainly," replied the barber.

Competency, and content, therefore, may in general, be considered as the basis of earthly happiness; and solitude, in many instances, favors both the one and the other.

Solitude not only refines the enjoyments of friendship, but enables us to acquire friends from whom nothing can alienate our souls, and to whose arms we never fly in vain.

The friends of Petrarch sometimes apologized to him for their long absence. "It is impossible for us," said they, "to follow your example; the life you lead at Vaucluse is contrary to human nature. In winter you sit like an owl in the chimney corner. In summer you are running incessantly about the fields." Petrarch smiled at these observations. "These people," said he, "consider the pleasures of the world as the supreme good; and cannot bear the idea of renouncing them. I have friends whose society is extremely agreeable to me: they are of all ages, and of every country. They have distinguished themselves both in the cabinet and in the field, and obtained high honors for their knowledge of the sciences. It is easy to gain access to them, for they are always at my service; and I admit them to my company, and dismiss them from it whenever I please. They are never troublesome, but immediately answer every question I ask them. Some relate to me the events of past ages, while others reveal to me the secrets of nature. Some teach me how to live, and others how to die. Some, by their vivacity, drive away my cares, and exhilarate my spirits; while others give fortitude to my mind, and teach me the important lesson how to restrain my desires, and to depend on myself. They open to me, in short, the various avenues of all the arts and sciences; and upon their information I safely rely in all emergencies. In return for all these services, they only ask me to accommodate them with a convenient chamber in some corner of my humble habitation, where they may repose in peace: for these friends are more delighted with the tranquillity of retirement, than with the tumults of society."

Love! the most precious gift of heaven,

> "The cordial drop Heav'n in our cup has thrown,
> To make the bitter load of life go down,"

appears to merit a distinguished rank among the advantages of solitude.

Love voluntarily unites itself with the aspect of beautiful nature. The view of a pleasing landscape makes the heart beat with the tenderest emotions. The lonely mountain and the silent grove increase the susceptibility of the female bosom, inspire the mind with rapturous enthusiasm, and, sooner or later, draw aside and subjugate the heart.

Women feel the pure and tranquil pleasures of rural life with a higher sensibility than men. They enjoy more exquisitely the beauties of a lonely walk, the freshness of a shady forest, and admire with higher ecstacy the charms of nature. Solitude is to them the school of true philosophy. In England, at least, where the face of the country is so beautiful, and where the taste of its inhabitants is hourly adding to it new embellishments, the love of rural solitude is certainly stronger in the women than the men. A nobleman who employs the day in riding over his estates or in following the hounds, does not enjoy the pleasures of rural life with the same delight as his lady, who devotes her time, in her romantic pleasure grounds, to needle work, or to the reading of some instructive, interesting work. In this happy country, indeed, where the people, in general, love the enjoyments of the mind, the calm of rural retirement is doubly valuable, and its delights more exquisite. The learning which has of late years so considerably increased among the ladies of Germany, is certainly to be attributed to their love of retirement: for, among those who pass their time in the country, we find much more true wit and rational sentiment, than among the *beaux esprits* of the metropolis.

Minds, indeed, apparently insensible in the atmosphere of a metropolis, unfold themselves with rapture in the country. This is the reason why the return of spring fills every tender breast with love. "What can more resemble love," says a celebrated German philosopher, "than the feeling with which my soul is inspired at the sight of this magnificent valley, thus illuminated by the setting sun!" Rousseau felt an inexpressible delight on viewing the first appearances of spring: the earliest blossoms of that charming season gave new life and vigor to his mind; the tenderest dispositions of his heart were awakened and augmented by the soft verdure it presented to his eyes; and the charms of his mistress were assimilated with the beauties that surrounded him on every side. The view of an extensive and pleasing prospect softened his sorrows; and he breathed his sighs with exquisite delight amidst the rising flowers of his garden, and the rich fruits of his orchard.

Lovers constantly seek the rural grove to indulge, in the tranquillity of retirement, the uninterrupted contemplation of the beloved object which forms the sole happiness of their lives. Of what importance to them are all the transactions of the world, or, indeed, any thing that does not tend to indulge the passion that fills their hearts? Silent groves, embowering glades, or the lonely borders of murmuring streams, where they may freely resign themselves to their fond reflections, are the only confidants of their souls. A lovely shepherdess, offering her fostering bosom to the infant she is nursing, while at her side her well-beloved partner sits dividing with her his morsel of hard black bread, is an hundred times more happy than all the fops of the town: for love inspires his mind, in the highest degree, with all that is elevated, delightful and affecting in nature; and warms the coldest bosoms with the greatest sensibility and the highest rapture.

Love's softest images spring up anew in solitude. The remembrance of these emotions which the first blush of conscious tenderness, the first gentle pressure of the hand, the first dread of interruption, create, recurs incessantly! Time, it is said, extinguishes the flame of love; but solitude renews the fire, and calls forth those agents which lie long concealed, and only wait a favorable moment to display their powers. The whole course of youthful feeling again beams forth; and the mind—delicious recollection!— fondly retracing the first affection of the heart, fills the bosom with an indelible sense of those high ecstacies which a connoisseur has said, with as much truth as energy, proclaim, for the first time, that happy discovery, that fortunate moment, when two lovers first perceive their mutual fondness.

Herder mentions a certain cast of people in Asia, whose mythology thus divided the felicities of eternity. "That men, after death, were, in the celestial regions, immediately the objects of female love during the course of a thousand years; first by tender looks, then by a balmy kiss, and afterwards, by immediate alliance."

It was this noble and sublime species of affection that Wieland, in the warmest moments of impassioned youth felt for an amiable, sensible, and beautiful lady of Zurich; for that extraordinary genius was perfectly satisfied, that the metaphysical effects of love, begin with the first sigh, and expire, to a certain degree, with the first kiss. I one day asked this young lady when it was that Wieland had saluted her for the first time? "Wieland," replied the amiable girl, "did not kiss my hand for the first time until four years after our acquaintance commenced."

Young persons, in general, however, do not, like Wieland, adopt the mystic refinements of love. Yielding to the sentiments which the passion inspires, and less acquainted with its metaphysical nature, they feel at an earlier age, in the tranquillity of solitude, that irresistible impulse to the union of the sexes which the God of nature has so strongly implanted in the human breast.

A lady who resided in great retirement, at a romantic cottage upon the banks of the lake of Geneva, had three innocent and lovely daughters. The eldest was about fourteen years of age, the youngest was about nine, when they were presented with a tame bird, which hopped and flew about the chamber the whole day, and formed the sole amusement and pleasure of their lives. Placing themselves on their knees, they offered, with unwearied delight, their little favorite, pieces of biscuit from their fingers, and endeavored, by every means, to induce him to fly to, and nestle in, their bosoms; but the bird, the moment he had got the biscuit, with cunning coyness eluded their hopes, and hopped away. The little favorite at length died. A year after this event, the youngest of the three sisters said to her mother, "Oh, I remember that dear little bird! I wish, mamma, you could procure me such a one to play with." "Oh! no," replied her elder sister, "I should like to have a little dog to play with better than any thing. I could catch a little dog, take him on my knee, hug him in my arms. A bird affords me no pleasure; he perches a little while on my finger, then flies away, and there is no catching him again: but a little dog, oh! what pleasure...."

I shall never forget the poor *religieuse* in whose apartment I found a breeding cage of canary birds, nor forgive myself for having burst into a fit of laughter at the discovery. It was, alas! the suggestion of nature; and who can resist what nature suggests? This mystic wandering of religious minds, this celestial epilepsy of love, this premature effect of solitude, is only the fond application of natural inclination raised superior to all others.

Absence and tranquillity appear so favorable to the indulgence of this pleasing passion, that lovers frequently quit the beloved object, to reflect in solitude on her charms. Who does not recollect to have read, in the Confessions of Rousseau, the story related by Madame de Luxemberg, of a lover who quitted the presence of his mistress, only that he might have the pleasure of writing to her. Rousseau replied to Madame de Luxemberg, that he wished he had been that man; and his wish was founded on a perfect knowledge of the passion: for who has ever been in love, and does not know that there are moments when the pen is capable of expressing the fine feelings of the heart with much greater effect than the voice, with its miserable organ of speech? The tongue, even in its happiest elocution, is never so persuasive as the speaking eyes, when lovers gaze with silent ecstacy on each other's charms.

Lovers not only express, but feel their passion with higher ecstacy and happiness in solitude than in any other situation. What fashionable lover ever painted his passion for a lovely mistress with such laconic tenderness and effect, as the village chorister of Hanover did on the death of a young and beautiful country girl with whom he was enamored, when, after erecting in the cemetery of the cathedral, a sepulchral stone to her memory, he carved, in an artless manner, the figure of a blooming rose on its front, and inscribed beneath it these words: *C'est ainsi qu'elle fut.*

It was at the feet of those rocks which overhung the celebrated retreat at Vaucluse, that Petrarch composed his finest sonnets to deplore the absence, or to complain of the cruelty of his beloved Laura. The Italians are of opinion, that when love inspired his muse, his poetry soared far beyond that of any poet who ever wrote before or since his time, either in the Greek, the Latin, or the Tuscan languages. "Ah! how soft and tender is this language of the heart!" they exclaim. "Petrarch alone was acquainted with its power: he has added to the three graces a fourth—the grace of delicacy."

Love, however, when indulged in rural solitude or amidst the romantic scenery of an ancient castle, and, assisted by the ardent imagination of impetuous youth, frequently assumes a more bold and violent character. Religious enthusiasm, blended with a saturnine disposition, forms, in effervescent minds, a sublime and extraordinary compound of the feelings of the heart. A youthful lover of this description, when deprived of the smiles of his mistress, takes his first declaration of love from the text of the apocalypse and thinks his passion an eternal melancholy; but when he is inclined to sharpen the dart within his breast, his inspired mind views in the beloved object the fairest model of divine perfection.

The lovers of this romantic cast, placed in some ancient solitary castle, soar far beyond the common tribe, and, as their ideas refine, their passions become proportionably sublime. Surrounded by stupendous rocks, and impressed by the awful stilness of the scene, the beloved youth is considered not merely as an amiable and virtuous man, but as a god. The inspired mind of the fond female fancies her bosom to be the sanctuary of love, and conceives her affection for the youthful idol of her heart to be an emanation from heaven: a ray of the Divine Presence. Ordinary lovers, without doubt, in spite of absence, unite their souls, write by every post, seize all occasions to converse with, or hear from, each other; but our more sublime and exalted female introduces into her romance of passion every butterfly she meets with, and all the feathered songsters of the groves; and, except in the object of her love, no longer sees any thing as it really is. Reason and sense no longer guide: the refinements of love direct all her movements; she tears the world from its poles, and the sun from its axis; and to prove that all she does is right, establishes for herself and her lover a new gospel, and a new system of morality.

A lover, separated, perhaps, forever, from a mistress who has made the most important sacrifices to his happiness; who was his only consolation in affliction, his only comfort in calamity; whose kindness supported his sinking fortitude; who remained his faithful and his only friend in dire adversity and domestic sorrow; seeks, as his sole resource, a slothful solitude. Nights passed in sleepless agonies; a distaste of life, a desire of death, an abhorrence of all society, and a love of dreary seclusion, drive him, day, after day, wandering, as chance may direct, though the most solitary retirements far from the hated traces of mankind. Were he, however, to wander from the Elbe to the lake of Geneva; were he to seek relief in the frozen confines of the north, or the burning regions of the west, to the utmost extremities of the earth or seas, he would still be like the hind described by Virgil:

> "Stung with the stroke and madding with the pain
>
> She wildly flies from wood to wood in vain;
>
> Shoots o'er the Cretan lawn with many a bound,
>
> The cleaving dart still rankling in the wound."

Petrarch, on returning to Vaucluse, felt with new and increasing stings the passion which perturbed his breast. Immediately on his arrival at this sequestered spot, the image of his beloved Laura incessantly haunted his imagination. He beheld her at all times, in every place, and under a thousand different forms. "Three times in the middle of the night when every door was closed, she appeared to me," says he, "at the feet of my bed, with a steadfast look, as if confident of the power of her charms. Fear spread a chilling dew over all my limbs. My blood thrilled through my veins towards my heart. If any one had then entered my apartment with a candle, they would have beheld me as pale as death, with every mark of terror on my face. Rising before the break of day, with trembling limbs, from my disordered bed, and hastily leaving my house, where every thing created alarm, I climbed to the summit of the rocks, and ran wildly through the woods, casting my eyes incessantly on every side, to see if the form which had haunted my repose, still pursued me. Alas! I could find no asylum. Places the most sequestered, where I fondly flattered myself that I should be alone, presented her continually to my mind; and I beheld her sometimes issuing from the hollow trunk of a tree, from the concealed source of a spring, or from the dark cavity of a broken rock. Fear rendered me insensible, and I neither know what I did, or where I went."

The heart of Petrarch was frequently stimulated by ideas of voluptuous pleasure, even among the rocks of Vaucluse, where he sought an asylum from love and Laura. He soon, however, banished sensuality from his mind, and, by refining his passion, acquired that vivacity and heavenly purity which breathes in every line of those immortal lyrics he composed among the rocks. But the city of Avignon, in which the object thus tenderly beloved resided, was not sufficiently distant from the place of his retreat, and he visited it too frequently. A passion indeed, like that which Petrarch felt, leaves the bosom, even when uncorrupted, totally incapable of tranquillity. It is a violent fever of the soul, which inflicts upon the body a complication of painful disorders. Let lovers, therefore, while they possess some control over the passion which fills their breasts, seat themselves on the borders of a river, and reflect that love, like the stream, sometimes precipitates itself with violence down the rocks; and sometimes flowing with soft tranquillity along the plain, meanders through meadows, and loses itself beneath the peaceful shades of solitary bowers.

The tranquillity of solitude, however, may, to a mind disposed to resign itself with humility to all the dispensations of heaven, be found not disadvantageous to the perturbations of love. A lover whom death has bereaved of the dear object of his affection, seeks only those places which his favorite inhabited; considers every other as desert and forlorn; and expects that death alone is able to stop the torrent of his tears. Such an indulgence of sorrow, however, cannot be called a resignation to the will of God. A lover of this description is attached solely to the irrecoverable object of his increasing sorrows. His distracted mind fondly hopes that she may still return; he thinks he hears her soft enchanting voice in every breeze; he sees her lovely form approaching, and opens his expecting arms to clasp her once again to his still throbbing breast. But he finds, alas! his hopes are vain: the fancy-breathing form eludes his grasp, and convinces him that the delightful vision was only the light and love-formed phantom of his sorrow-sickened mind. A sad remembrance of her departed spirit is the only comfort of his lingering life: he flies to the tomb where her mortal remains were deposited, plants roses round her shrine, waters them with his tears, cultivates them with the tenderest care, kisses them as emblems of her blushing cheeks, and tastes, with sighing transports, their balmy fragrance as the fancied odor of her ruby lips.

It must afford infinite pleasure to every philosophic mind, to reflect on the victory which the virtuous Petrarch gained over the passion that assailed his heart. During his retreat into Italy from love and Laura, his friends in France used every endeavor to induce him to return. One of them wrote to him:—"What demon possesses you;—How could you quit a country in which you indulged all the propensities of youth, and where the graceful figure which you formerly adorned with so much care, procured you such unbounded admiration?—How can you live thus exiled from Laura, whom you love with so much tenderness, and whose heart is so deeply afflicted by your absence?"

Petrarch replied: "Your anxiety is vain: I am resolved to continue where I am. I ride here safely at anchor; and all the hurricanes of eloquence shall never drive me from it. How then can you expect to persuade me to change this resolution, merely by placing before my eyes the deviations of my youth which I ought to forget; by describing an illicit passion which left me no other resource than a precipitate flight; and by extolling the meretricious advantages of a handsome person, which too long occupied my attention. These are follies I must no longer think of. I am now rapidly approaching toward the last goal on the course of life. Objects more serious and important now occupy my thoughts. God forbid, that, listening to your flattering observations, I should again throw myself into the snares of love, again put on a yoke which so severely galled me!—The natural levity of youth apologizes, in some degree, for the indiscretions it creates; but I should despise myself, if I could now be tempted to revisit either the bower of love, or the theatre of ambition. Your suggestions, however, have produced a proper effect; for I consider them as the oblique censures of a friend upon my past misconduct. The solicitudes of the gay and busy world no longer disturb my mind; for my heart has tenaciously rooted all its fibres in this delightful solitude, where I rove at large, free and unconstrained, without inquietude or care. In summer I repose upon the verdant turf beneath the shade of some embowering tree, or saunter along the enamelled boarders of a cool, refreshing stream. At the approach of autumn I seek the woods, and join the muses' train. This mode of life is surely preferable to a life at court, where nothing but disgusting jealousies and corroding cares exist. I have now, in short, no wish, except that, when death relieves me both from pleasure and from pain, I may recline my head upon the bosom of a friend, whose eyes, while he performs the last office of closing mine, will drop a deploring tear upon my departing spirit, and convey my remains, with friendly care, to a decent tomb in my native country."

These were the sentiments of *the philosopher*: but, after a short interval *the man* returned once again to the city of Avignon, and only visited his retreat at Vaucluse occasionally.

Petrarch, however, by these continued endeavors to subdue the violence of his passion, acquired a sublimity and richness of imagination, which distinguished his character, and gave him an ascendency over the age in which he lived, greater than any of the literati have since attained. To use the expression of the poet, he was capable of passing, with the happiest facility,

"From grave to gay, from lively to severe:"

and was enabled, as occasion required, to conceive the boldest enterprises, and to execute them with the most heroic courage. He who languished, sighed, and even wept with unmanly softness, at the feet of his mistress, breathing only the tender and affectionate language of gentle love, no sooner turned his thoughts toward the transactions of Rome, than he assumed a higher tone, and not only wrote, but acted with all the strength and spirit of the Augustan age. Monarchs have relinquished the calls of hunger, and the charms of rest, to indulge the tender luxuries his love-lorn muse afforded. But at a more advanced age he was no longer a sighing minstrel, chaunting amorous verses to a relentless fair; he was no longer an effeminate slave, that kissed the chains of an imperious mistress, who treated him with disdain: he became a zealous republican, who spread by his writings the spirit of liberty throughout Italy, and sounded a loud alarm against tyranny and tyrants. Great as a statesman, profound and judicious as a public minister, he was consulted in the most important political transactions of Europe, and frequently employed in the most arduous and difficult negotiations. Zealously active in the cause of humanity, he anxiously endeavored, on occasions, to extinguish the torch of discord. The greatest princes, conscious of his extraordinary genius, solicited his company, and endeavored, by listening to his precepts, to learn the noble art of rendering their countries respectable, and their people happy.

These traits of Petrarch's character clearly evince that, oppressed as he was by the passion of love, he derived great advantages from solitude. The retirement at Vaucluse was not, as is commonly imagined, a pretence to be nearer the person of Laura, for Laura resided altogether at Avignon; but a means of avoiding the frown of his mistress, and of flying from the contagion of a corrupt court. Seated in his little garden, which was situated at the foot of a lofty mountain, and surrounded by a rapid stream, his soul rose superior to the adversities of his fate. His disposition, indeed, was naturally restless and unquiet; but in his tranquil moments, a sound judgment, joined to an exquisite sensibility, enabled him to enjoy the delights of solitude with singular advantage; and to find in his retreat at Vaucluse, the temple of peace, the residence of calm repose, and a safe harbor against all the tempests of the soul.

The flame of love, therefore, although it cannot be entirely extinguished, may be greatly purified and refined by solitude. Man indeed, ought not to extirpate the passions which the God of nature has planted in the human heart, but to direct them to their proper ends.

To avoid such miseries as Petrarch endured, the pleasures of retirement should be shared with some amiable female, who, better than the cold precepts of philosophy, will beguile or banish, by the charms of conversation, all the cares and torments of life.

It has been said by a very sensible author, that "the presence of one thinking being like ourselves, whose bosom glows with sympathy, and whose affection we possess, so far from destroying the advantages of solitude, renders them more favorable. If, like me you owe your happiness to the fond attention of a wife, you will soon be induced, by her kindness, by her tender and unreserved communication of every sentiment of her mind, every feeling of her heart, to forget the society of the world; and your happiness will be as pleasingly diversified, as the employments and vicissitudes of your lives."

The orator who speaks so eloquently must have felt with exquisite sensibility the pleasures he describes; "Here," says he, "every kind expression is remembered; the emotions of one heart correspond with those of the other; every thought is treasured up; every testimony of affection is returned; the happy pair enjoy in each other's company all the pleasures of the mind; and there is no felicity which does not communicate itself to their hearts. To beings thus united by the sincerest affection, and the closest friendship, every thing that is said or done, every wish, and every event, becomes mutually important. No jealous fears, no envious stings, disturb their happiness; faults are pointed out with cautious tenderness and good nature; looks bespeak the inclinations of the soul; every wish and every desire is anticipated; every view and intention assimilated; and, the sentiments of one, conforming to those of the other, each rejoices with cordiality at the smallest advantage which the other acquires."

Thus it is that the solitude which we share with an amiable object produces tranquillity, satisfaction, and heartfelt joy; and makes the humblest cottage a dwelling place of the purest pleasure.

Love, in the shades of retirement, while the mind and the heart are in harmony with each other, inspires the noblest sentiments; raises the understanding to the highest sphere of intellect: fills the bosom with increased benevolence; destroys all the seeds of vice, and meliorates and extends all the virtues. By its delightful influence the attack of ill-humor is resisted; the violence of our passions abated; the bitter cup of human affliction sweetened; all the injuries of the world alleviated; and the sweetest flowers plentifully strewed along the thorny paths of life. Every unhappy sufferer, whether the malady be of the body or the mind, derives from this source extraordinary comfort and consolation. At a time, alas! when every thing displeased me, when every object was disgusting, when my sufferings had destroyed all the energy and vigor of my soul, when grief had shut from my streaming eyes the beauties of nature, and rendered the whole universe a dreary tomb, the kind attentions of a wife were capable of conveying a secret charm, a silent consolation to my mind. Oh! nothing can render the bowers of retirement so serene and comfortable, or can so sweetly soften all our woes, as a conviction that woman is not indifferent to our fate.

Solitude, it is true, will not completely heal every wound which this imperious passion is capable of inflicting on the human heart; but it teaches us to endure our pains without wishing for relief, and enables us to convert them into soft sorrow and plaintive grief.

Both sexes in early youth, but particularly females from fifteen to eighteen years of age, who possess high sensibilities, and lively imaginations, generally feel during the solitude of rural retirement, a soft and pleasing melancholy, when their bosoms begin to heave with the first propensities of love. They wander every where in search of a beloved object, and sigh for one alone, long before the heart is fixed in its affection, or the mind conscious of its latent inclination. I have frequently observed this disposition unaccompanied by any symptom of ill health. It is an original malady. Rousseau felt its influence at Vevay, upon the borders of the lake of Geneva. "My heart," says he, "rushed with ardor from my bosom into a thousand innocent felicities; and melting into tenderness, I sighed and wept like a child. How frequently, stopping to indulge my feelings, and seating myself on a piece of broken rock, did I amuse myself with seeing my tears drop into the stream!"

Retirement, however, is not equally favorable to every species of affliction. Some bosoms are so exquisitely alive to the sense of misfortune, that the indelible remembrance of the object of their affection preys upon their minds: the reading of a single line written by the hand they loved, freezes their blood; the very sight of the tomb which has swallowed up the remains of all their soul held dear, is intolerable to their eyes. On such beings, alas! the heavens smile in vain: to them the new-born flowers and the twittering groves, proclaiming the approach of spring and the regeneration of vegetable nature, bring no charms; the garden's variegated hues irritate their feelings; and the silent retreats, from which they once expected consolation, only increase their pains. Such refined and exquisite feelings, the offspring of warm and generous passion, are real misfortunes; and the malady they engender requires to be treated with the mildest attention and the tenderest care.

But to minds of softer temper solitude possesses many powerful charms, although the losses they deplore are equally great. Such characters feel, indeed, a sense of their misfortune in its utmost possible extent, but they soften its acuteness by yielding to the natural mildness of their dispositions: they plant upon the fatal tomb the weeping willow and the ephemeral rose; they erect *mausolea*; compose funeral dirges; and render the very emblems of death, the means of consolation. Their hearts are continually occupied by the idea of those whom their eyes deplore; and they exist under the sensations of the truest and most sincere sorrow, in a kind of middle state between earth and heaven. This species of sorrow is of the happiest kind. Far be it from me to suppose it in the least degree affected. But I call such characters happy mourners; because, from the very frame and texture of their constitutions, grief does not destroy the energy of their minds, but permits them to find consolation in those things which, to minds differently constructed, would create aversion. They feel a heavenly joy in pursuing employments which preserve the memory of those who are the subjects of their sorrow.

Solitude will enable the heart to vanquish the most painful sense of adversity, provided the mind will generously lend its aid, and fix its attention to a different object. If men think there is any misfortune from which they have no other resource than despair or death they deceive themselves; for despair is no resource. Let such men retire to their studies, and there seriously trace out a series of important and settled truths, and their tears will no longer fall; but the weight of their misfortunes will grow light, and sorrow fly from their breasts.

Solitude, by encouraging the enjoyments of the heart, by promoting domestic felicity, and by creating a taste for rural scenery, subdues impatience, and drives away ill-humor. Impatience is a stifled anger, which men silently manifest by looks and gestures, and weak minds ordinarily reveal by a shower of complaints. A grumbler is never further from his proper sphere than when he is in company; solitude is his only asylum. Ill-humor is an uneasy and insupportable condition, which the soul frequently falls into when soured by a number of those petty vexations which we daily experience in every step of our progress through life; but we need only to shut the door against improper and disagreeable intrusions, to avoid this scourge of happiness.

Vexations, indeed, of every kind, are much sooner quieted in the silence of retirement than in the noise of the world. A cheerful disposition, a placid temper, and well-regulated passions, will prevent worldly vexations from interrupting our happiness. By these attainments, the deepest melancholy, and most settled uneasiness of life, have been frequently banished from the heart. It is true, that the progress in this case is much more rapid in women than in men. The mind of a lively female flies immediately to happiness, while that of a melancholy man still creeps on with pain: the yielding bosoms of the fair are easily elevated or depressed. These effects, it is true, may be produced by means less abstracted than solitude; by any thing that strikes the senses, and penetrates the heart. Men, on the contrary, augment the disease, and fix it more firmly in the bosom, by brooding over its cause and consequences, and are obliged to apply the most efficacious remedies, with unshaken constancy, to effect a cure; for feeble prescriptions are, in such cases, of no avail. The only chance, indeed, of success, is by exerting every endeavor to place the body under the regimen of the mind. Vigorous minds frequently banish the most inveterate evils, or form a powerful shield against all the darts of fate, and, by braving every danger, drive away those feelings by which others are irritated and destroyed; they boldly turn their eyes from what things are, to what they ought to be; and with determined resolution support the bodies they are designed to animate; while weak minds surrender every thing committed to their care.

The soul, however, always follows what is most agreeable to its ruling passion. Worldly men generally delight in gaming, feasting, and debauchery; while those who are fond of solitude feel, from a consciousness of its advantages, no enjoyments equal to those its peaceful shades afford.

I now conclude my reflections upon the advantages of Solitude to *the Heart*. May they give greater currency to useful sentiments, to consolatory truths, and contribute in some degree to diffuse the enjoyment of a happiness which is so much within our reach!

Chapter IV
The General Advantages of Retirement

Retirement engages the affections of men whenever it holds up a picture of tranquillity to their view.

The doleful and monotonous sound of the clock of a sequestered monastery, the silence of nature in a still night, the pure air on the summit of a high mountain, the thick darkness of an aged forest, the sight of a temple fallen into ruins, inspire the soul with a soft melancholy, and banish all recollection of the world and its concerns.

The man who cannot hold a friendly correspondence with his own heart; who derives no comfort from the reflections of his mind; who dreads the idea of meditation, and is fearful of passing a single moment with himself, looks with equal dread on solitude and on death. He endeavors to enjoy all the voluptuousness which the world affords; drains the pernicious cup of pleasure to its dregs; and, until the dreadful moment approaches when he beholds his nerves shattered, and all the powers of his soul destroyed, has not the courage to make the delayed confession, "I am tired of the world and all its idle follies!"

The legions of fantastic fashions to which a man of pleasure is obliged to sacrifice his time, impair the rational faculties of his mind, and destroy the native energies of his soul. Forced continually to lend himself to the performance of a thousand little trifles, a thousand mean absurdities, he becomes by habit frivolous and absurd. The face of things no longer wears its true and genuine aspect; and his depraved taste loses all relish for rational entertainment or substantial pleasure. The infatuation seizes on his brain, and his corrupted heart teems with idle fancies and vain imaginations.

The inevitable consequences of this ardent pursuit of entertainments and diversions are langor and dissatisfaction. He has drained the cup of pleasure to the last drop, who is at length obliged to confess that all his hopes are fled; who finds disappointment and disgust mingled with every enjoyment; who feels astonished at his own insensibility, and who no longer possesses the magic of the enchantress, imagination, to gild and decorate the scene, calls in vain to his assistance the daughters of sensuality and intemperance: their caresses can no longer delight his dark and melancholy mind: the soft and syren song of luxury no longer can dispel the cloud of discontent that hovers round his head.

Behold that debilitated weak old man running after pleasures he can no longer enjoy. The airs of gayety which he affects render him ridiculous; his attempts to shine expose him to derision; his endeavors to display the wit and eloquence of youth betray him into the garrulity of old age. His conversation, filled with repetition and tiresome narrative, creates disgust, and only forces the smile of pity from the lips of his youthful rivals. To the eye of wisdom, however, who observed him through all the former periods of his life, sparkling in the noisy circles of extravagance and vice, his character always appeared the same.

The wise man, in the midst of the most tumultuous pleasures, frequently retires within himself, and silently compares what he might do with what he is doing. Surrounded by, and even when accidentally engaged in, the excesses of intoxication, he associates only with those warm and generous souls whose highly elevated minds are drawn toward each other by the most virtuous inclinations and sublime sentiments. The silent retreat of the mind within itself, has more than once given birth to enterprizes of the greatest importance and utility; and it is not difficult to imagine, that some of the most celebrated actions of mankind were first inspired among the sounds of music, or conceived amidst the mazes of the dance. Sensible and elevated minds never commune more closely with themselves than in those places of public resort in which the low and vulgar, surrendering themselves to illusion and caprice, become incapable of reflection, and blindly suffer themselves to be overwhelmed by the surrounding torrent of folly and distraction.

The unceasing pursuit of sensual enjoyment is merely a mean used by the votaries of worldly pleasure, of flying from themselves; they seize with avidity upon any object that promises to occupy the present hour agreeably, and provide entertainment for the day that is passing over their heads. To such characters the man who can invent hour after hour new schemes of pleasure and open day after day fresh sources of amusement, is a valuable companion indeed; he is their best, their only friend. Are then these lazy and luxurious votaries of sensual pleasures destitute of those abilities which might prevent this sacrifice of time, and, if properly exerted, afford them relief? Certainly not. But, having been continually led from object to object in the pursuit of pleasure, the assistance of others has habitually become the first want and greatest necessity of their lives: they have insensibly lost all power of acting for themselves, and depend, for every object they see, for every sensation they feel, for every sentiment they entertain, on those by whom they are attended. This is the reason why the rich, who are seldom acquainted with any other pleasures than those of sense, are, in general, the most miserable of mankind.

The nobility and courtiers of France think their enjoyments appear vain and ridiculous only to those who have not the opportunity of partaking in them; but I am of a different opinion. Returning one Sunday from Trianon to Versailles, I perceived at a distance a number of people assembled upon the terrace of the castle; and on a nearer approach, I beheld Louis XV. surrounded by his court, at the windows of his palace. A man very richly dressed, with a large pair of branching antlers fastened upon his head, whom they called the stag, was pursued by about a dozen others who composed the pack. The pursued and the pursuers leaped into the great canal, scrambled out again, and ran wildly round and round, amidst the acclamations of the assembly, who loudly clapped their hands to testify their delight, and to encourage the diversion. "What can all this mean?" said I to a French gentleman who stood near me. "Sir," he replied, with a very serious countenance, "it is for the entertainment of the court." The most obscure and indigent individuals may certainly be much happier than these masters of mankind with their melancholy slaves and miserable entertainments.

Direful condition! Is there then no occupation whatsoever, no useful employment, no rational recreation sufficiently high and dignified for such characters?—Are they reduced to the melancholy condition of not being able to perform one good and virtuous action during the intervals of suspended pleasure? Can they render no services to friendship, to their country, to themselves? Are there no poor and miserable beings to whose bosom they might afford charitable comfort and relief? Is it, in short, impossible for such characters in any way to improve themselves in wisdom or in virtue?

The powers of the human mind are of greater extent than is generally imagined. He who, either from taste or necessity, exercises them frequently, soon finds that the highest felicities of which our nature is capable, reside entirely within ourselves. The wants of life are, for the greater part, merely artificial; and although sensual objects contribute most efficaciously to our happiness and delight, it is not because they are indispensably necessary for this purpose, but because they have been rendered desirable by habit; and, from the pleasures they produce, we flatter ourselves that they are absolutely necessary to our felicity. If, however, we had fortitude to resist their charms, and courage to seek our happiness in ourselves, we should frequently find in our own bosoms a greater variety of resources than all the objects of sense are capable of affording.

Amusements, indeed, may sometimes be found in those places to which the sexes resort merely to see and to be seen. The eye may be occasionally gratified by the sight of objects really agreeable; the ear may listen to observations truly flattering. Lively thoughts and sensible remarks now and then prevail. Characters equally amiable and interesting occasionally mix among the group. We may form acquaintance with men of distinguished merit, whom we should not otherwise have had an opportunity of knowing; and meet with women of amiable qualities, and irreproachable conduct, whose refined conversation ravishes the ear with a delight equal to that with which their exquisite beauty captivates the heart. But by what a number of painful sensations must the chance of receiving these pleasures be purchased! Those whom reason or disgust restrain from mixing in the idle dissipations of life, cannot see without a sigh, the gay conceit, the airy confidence, the blind arrogance, and the bold loquacity, with which these votaries of worldly pleasure proclaim a felicity which is almost invariably deceitful; nor observe without a sigh, the extravagant joy of so many great men, and the absurd airs of so many gray-headed children.

Honor, fame, and pleasure are conceived to accompany an invitation to the board of luxury; although disease, with leaden sceptre, is known to preside; and reproach and calumny are indiscriminately cast upon the purest characters. But he who feels the least energy of mind, turns with aversion from all society which tends to weaken its effect; and finds the simplest fare, enjoyed with freedom and content amidst a happy and affectionate family, ten thousand times more agreeable than the rarest dainty, and the richest wine, with a society where he must sit ceremoniously silent in compliment to some reputed wit, from whose lips nothing but absurdities and nonsense proceed.

The spiritless and crowded societies of the world, where a round of low and trifling amusements fills the hour of entertainment, and where to display a pomp of dress and levity of manners is the only ambition, may afford some pleasure to those light and empty minds who are impatient of the weight of idleness; but the wise man, who occasionally resorts to them in search of rational conversation or temporary amusement, and only finds a dull unvaried jargon, and a tiresome round of compliments, will turn with aversion from these temples of false delight, and exclaim, in the language of the poet,

> "I envy none their pageantry and show,
>
> I envy none the gilding of their wo.
>
> Give me, indulgent gods! with mind serene,
>
> And guiltless heart, to range the sylvan scene;

No splendid poverty, no smiling care,

No well-bred hate or servile grandeur there:

The pleasing objects useful thoughts suggest;

The sense is ravish'd and the soul is blest:

On every thorn, delightful wisdom glows,

In every rill a sweet instruction flows."

True social pleasure is founded on unlimited confidence, on an affectionate and reciprocal interchange of sentiment and opinions. A tender, faithful, refined, and rational friendship, renders the pleasures of the world spiritless and disgusting. How joyfully do we disencumber ourselves from the shackles of society, for that close and sublime intercourse in which our inclinations are free, our feelings generous, our sentiments unbiassed; where a mutuality of thought and action, of pleasure and of pains uninterruptedly prevail; where the gentle hand of love conducts us along the paths of truth and virtue; where every thought is anticipated before it escapes from the lips; where advice, consolation, and succor, are reciprocally given and received in all the accidents and in all the misfortunes of life! The soul, touched by the charms of friendship, springs from its apathy and dejection, and views the enlivening beam of hope awakening it to activity. The happy pair, casting a retrospective glance on the time passed, mutually exclaim with the tenderest emotions, "Oh the delights that we have already experienced!—Oh the joys that we have already felt!" If the tear of affliction steal down the cheek of the one, the other with affection wipes it tenderly away. The sorrows of one are felt with equal sensibility by the other: and what sorrow will not an intercourse of hearts so closely and affectionately united, entirely subdue!—Day after day they communicate to each other all they have seen, all they have heard, all that they feel, and every thing that they know. Time flies before them on his swiftest pinions. They are never tired of each other's company and conversation. The only misfortune they fear, the greatest indeed they can possibly experience, is the misfortune of being separated by occasional absence or untimely death.

But human happiness is continually exposed to interruption. At the very moment alas; when we vainly think ourselves the most secure, fate, by a sudden blow, strikes its unhappy victim even in our arms. All the pleasure of life then seems forever extinguished, every object alarms our mind, and every place seems desert and forlorn. In vain are our arms extended to embrace our loved, though lost companion; in vain do we invoke her return. Her well known step still seems to beat upon the listening ear, and promise her approach; but suspended sense returns, and the delusive sounds are heard no more. A death-like silence reigns around, and involves us in the shades of dreary solitude, unconscious of every thing but our bleeding hearts. Wearied and dejected, we imagine ourselves no longer capable of loving or of being beloved; and life without love, to the heart that has once felt its pleasures, is more terrible than death. So sudden a transition from the highest happiness to the deepest misery overpowers the mind. No kind friend appears to assuage our sufferings, or seems capable of forming an adequate idea of our distress. The pangs, indeed, which such a loss inflicts, cannot be conceived, unless they have been felt. The only consolation of the unhappy sufferer is to live in solitude, and his only wish to die alone. But it is under circumstances like these that solitude enjoys its greatest triumph, and the afflicted sufferer receives the greatest benefits; for there is no sorrow, however great, no pang, however powerful, that it will not, when wisely indulged, at first soften, and at length subdue. The remedy which solitude "administers to a mind diseased," is slow and gradual; for the art of living alone requires much experience, is subject to so many casualties, and depends so materially upon the temperament of the patient, that it is necessary we should attain a complete maturity before any great advantages can be derived from it. But he who is able to throw off the galling yoke of prejudice, and possesses a natural esteem and fondness for retirement, will not be embarrassed as to the choice he ought to make under such circumstances. Indifferent to external objects, and averse from the dissipations of the world, he will rely on the powers of his mind, and will never be less alone than when he is in the company of himself.

Men of genius are frequently condemned to employments as disagreeable to the turn and temper of their minds, as the most nauseous medicine must be to an empty stomach. Confined to toil on a dry and disgusting subject, fixed to a particular spot, and harassed by subordinate duties, they relinquish all expectation of tranquillity on this side the grave. Deprived of enjoying the common pleasures of nature, every object increases their disgust. "It is not for us," they exclaim, "that the youthful zephyrs call forth the budding foliage with their caressing breath; that the feathered choir chant in enlivening strains their rural songs; that the verdant meadows are decked with fragrant flowers." But set these complainers free, give them liberty and leisure to think for themselves, and the enthusiasm of their minds will soon regenerate, and soar into the highest regions of intellectual happiness, with the bold wing and penetrating eye of the bird of Jove.

If solitude be capable of dissipating the afflictions of persons thus circumstanced, what may not be expected from its influence on those who are enabled to retire, at pleasure, to its friendly shades, and who have no other wish than to enjoy pure air and domestic felicity! When Antisthenes was asked what advantages philosophy had afforded him, he answered, "*It has taught me to subdue myself."* Pope says, he never laid his head upon his pillow, without acknowledging that the most important lesson of life is to learn the art of being happy within ourselves. And it seems to me that we shall all find what Pope looked for, when home is our content, and every thing about us, even to the dog and the cat, partakes of our affection.

Health is certainly essential to happiness, and yet there are circumstances and situations, under which the privation of it may be attended with tranquillity.

How frequently have I returned thanks to God, when indisposition has prevented me from going abroad, and enabled me to recruit my weakened powers in solitude and silence! Obliged to drag through the streets of the metropolis day after day during a number of years, feeble in constitution, weak in limbs; susceptible, on feeling the smallest cold, to the same sensation as if knives were separating the flesh from the bone; continually surrounded, in the course of my profession, with the most afflicting sorrows; it is not surprising that I should thank the Almighty with tears of gratitude, on experiencing even the relief which a confinement by indisposition procured. A physician, if he possesses sensibility, must, in his anxiety to relieve the sufferings of others, frequently forget his own. But, alas! how frequently must he feel all the horrors of his situation, when he is summoned to attend patients whose maladies are beyond the reach of medicine! Under such circumstances, the indisposition which excuses my attendance, and leaves me the powers of thought, affords me comparatively a sweet repose; and, provided I am not disturbed by the polite interruptions of ceremonious visiters, I enjoy a pleasing solitude. One single day passed undisturbed at home in literary leisure, affords to the mind more real pleasure than all the circles of fashionable entertainment are able to bestow.

The fear of being alone is no longer felt either by the young or old, whenever the mind has acquired the power of employing itself in some useful or agreeable study. Ill humor may be banished by adopting a regular course of reading. Books, indeed, cannot be inspected without producing a beneficial effect, provided we always read with a pen or pencil in our hand, and note down the new ideas that may occur, or the observations which confirm the knowledge we before possessed; for reading becomes not only useless, but fatiguing, unless we apply the information it affords either to our own characters, or to those of other men. This habit, however, may be easily acquired; and then books become one of the most safe and certain antidotes to lassitude and discontent. By this means a man becomes his own companion, and finds his best and most cheerful friend in his own heart.

Pleasures of this kind certainly surpass in a great degree all those which result merely from the indulgence of the senses. The pleasures of the mind, generally speaking, signify sublime meditation, the profound deductions of reason, and the brilliant effusions of the imagination; but there are also others, for the perfect enjoyment of which, neither extensive knowledge nor extraordinary talents are necessary. Such are the pleasures which result from active labor; pleasures equally within the reach of the ignorant and learned, and not less exquisite than those which result from the mind. Manual exertions, therefore, ought never to be despised. I am acquainted with gentlemen who understand the mechanism of their watches, who are able to work as painters, locksmiths, carpenters, and who are not only possessed of the tools and implements of every trade, but know how to use them. Such men never feel the least disquietude from the want of society, and are in general the happiest characters in existence.

Mental pleasures are within the reach of all persons who, free, tranquil, and affectionate, are contented with themselves, and at peace with their fellow-creatures. The mind contemplates the pranks of school, the sprightly aberrations of our boyish days, the wanton stories of early youth, our plays and pastimes, and all the little hopes and fears of infancy, with fond delight. Oh! with what approving smiles and soft regret, the aged cast their eyes upon those happy times when youthful inclination prompted all their actions, when every enterprise was undertaken with lively vigor, and executed with undaunted courage; when difficulties were sought merely for the purpose of surmounting them! Let us compare what we were formerly with what we are at present; or rather, by giving our thoughts a freer range, reflect on the various events we have experienced or observed; upon the means that the Almighty employs to raise or sink the prosperity of empires; upon the rapid progress made, even in our time, in every art and science; upon the diffusion of useful knowledge, and the destruction of dangerous prejudices; upon the empire which barbarism and superstition have gained, notwithstanding the exertions of genius and reason to prevent them; upon the sublime power of the human mind and its inefficient productions; and languor will instantly disappear, and tranquillity, peace, and good humor prevail.

Thus advantage may in solitude be attained and relished at every period of our lives; at the most advanced age, as well as during the vigor of youth. He who to an unbroken constitution joins a free and contented mind, and assiduously cultivates the powers of his understanding, will, if his heart be innocent, at all times enjoy the purest and most unalterable pleasures. Employment animates all the functions of the soul, and calls forth their highest energies. It is the secret consciousness which every person of a lively imagination possesses, of the powers of the mind, and the dignity they are capable of attaining, that creates the noble anxiety and ardor, which carries their efforts to the sublimest heights. But if, either by duty or situation, we maintain too close an intercourse with society, if we are obliged, in spite of inclination, to submit to frivolous and fatiguing dissipations, it is only by quitting the tumult, and entering into silent meditation, that we feel that effervescence, that desire to break from bondage, to fly from past errors, and avoid in future every noisy and tumultuous pleasure.

The mind never feels with more energy and satisfaction that it lives, that it is rational, great, active, free, and immortal, than during those moments in which it excludes idle and impertinent intruders.

Of all the vexations of life, there are none so insupportable, as those insipid visits, those annoying partialities, which occupy the time of frivolous and fashionable characters. "My thoughts," says Rousseau, "will only come when they please, and not when I choose:" and therefore the intrusions of strangers, or of mere acquaintances, were always extremely odious to him. It was for this reason alone that this extraordinary character, who seldom experienced an hour of tranquillity, felt such indignation against the importunate civilities and empty compliments of common conversation, whilst he enjoyed the rational intercourse of sensible and well-informed minds with the highest delight. How frequently are the brightest beams of intellect obscured by associating with low and little minds! How frequently do the soundest understandings become frivolous, by keeping frivolous company! For, although these bright beams are immediate emanations from the Deity on the mind of man, they must be matured by meditation and reflection, before they can give elevation to genius, and consistency to character.

Virtues to which the mind cannot rise even when assisted by the most advantageous intercourse, are frequently the fruits of solitude. Deprived for ever of the company and conversation of those whom we love and esteem, we endeavor to charm the uneasy void by every effort in our power; but while love and friendship lead us by the hand, and cherish us by their care, we lean incessantly on their bosoms, and remain inert. Solitude, were it for this reason alone, is indispensably necessary to the human character; for when men are enabled to depend on themselves alone, the soul, tossed about by the tempest of life, acquires new vigor; learns to bear with constancy, or avoid with address, those dangerous rocks on which vulgar minds are inevitably wrecked; and discovers continually new resources, by which the mind resists, with stoic courage, the rigors of its fate.

Weak minds always conceive it most safe to adopt the sentiments of the multitude. They never venture to express an opinion upon any subject until the majority have decided; and blindly follow the sentiments of the many, whether upon men or things, without troubling themselves to inquire who are right, or on which side truth preponderates. A love of equity and truth, indeed, is seldom found, except in those who have no dread of solitude. Men of dissipation never protect the weak, or avenge the oppressed. If the various and powerful hosts of knaves and fools are your enemies; if you have been injured in your property by injustice, or traduced in your fame by calumny, you must not fly for protection and redress to men of light and dissipated characters; for they are merely the organs of error, and the conduit pipes of prejudice.

The knowledge of ourselves is in solitude more easily and effectually acquired than in any other situation; for we there live in habits of the strictest intimacy with our own bosoms. It is certainly possible for men to be deliberate and wise, even amidst all the tumultuous folly of the world, especially if their principles be well fixed before they enter on the stage of life; but integrity is undoubtedly more easily preserved in the innocent simplicity of solitude, than in the corrupted intercourses of society. In the world how many men please only by their vices! How many profligate villains, and unprincipled adventurers of insinuating manners, are well received only because they have learnt the art of administering to the follies, the weaknesses, and the vices of others! The mind, intoxicated with the fumes of that incense which artful flattery is continually offering to it, is rendered incapable of justly appreciating the characters of men. On the contrary, we truly discover in the silence of solitude, the inward complexion of the heart; and learn not only what the characters of men are, but what in truth and nature they ought to be.

How many new and useful discoveries may be made by occasionally forcing ourselves from the vortex of the world, and retiring to the calm enjoyments of study and reflection! To accomplish this end, it is only necessary to commence seriously with our hearts, and to examine our actions with impartiality. The worldly-minded man, indeed, has reason to avoid this self-examination, for the result would in all probability be painful to his feelings; as he who only judges of himself by the flattering opinions which others may have expressed of his character, will, in such a scrutiny, behold with surprise that he is the miserable slave of habit and public opinion; submitting himself with scrupulous exactness, and the best possible grace, to the tyranny of fashion and established ceremony; never venturing to oppose their influence, however ridiculous and absurd it may be; and obsequiously following the example of others, without daring to resist pursuits which every one seems so highly to approve. He will perceive, that almost all his thoughts and actions are engendered by a base fear of himself, or arise from a servile complaisance to others; that he only seeks to flatter the vanities, and indulge the caprices of his superiors, and becomes the contemptible minister of these men, without daring to offer them the smallest contradiction, or hazard an opinion that is likely to give them the least displeasure. Whoever, with calm consideration, views this terrifying picture, will feel, in the silent emotions of his heart, the necessity of occasionally retiring into solitude, and seeking society with men of nobler sentiments and purer principles.

Let every one, therefore, who wishes to think with dignity, or live with ease, seek the retreats of solitude, and enter into a friendly intercourse with his own heart. How small a portion of true philosophy, with an enlightened understanding, will render it humble and compliant! But in the mists of prejudice, dazzled by the intellectual glimmer of false lights, every one mistakes the true path, and seeks for happiness in the shades of darkness, and in the labyrinths of obscurity. The habits of retirement and tranquillity can alone enable us to make a just estimate of men and things, and it is by renouncing all the prepossessions which the corruptions of society have implanted in the mind, that we make the first advances toward the restoration of reason, and the attainment of felicity.

We have hitherto only pointed out one class of the general advantages which may be derived from rational solitude, but there are many others which apply still more closely to men's business and bosoms. Who, alas! is there that has not experienced its comforting influence in the keenest adversities of life? Who is there that does not seek relief from its friendly shades in the langors of convalescence, in the pangs of affliction, and even in that distressful moment when death deprives us of those whose company was the charm and solace of our lives? Happy are they who know the advantages of a religious retirement, of that holy rest in which the virtues rivet themselves more closely to the soul, and in which every man, when he is on the bed of death, devoutly wishes he had lived.

But these advantages become more conspicuous, when we compare the manner of thinking which employs the mind of a solitary philosopher with that of a worldly sensualist; the tiresome tumultuous life of the one, with the ease and tranquillity of the other; the horrors which disturb the death bed of vice, with the calm sigh which accompanies the expiring soul of virtue. This is the awful moment in which we feel how important it is to commune morally with ourselves, and religiously with our Creator; to enable us to bear the sufferings of life with dignity, and the pains of death with ease.

The sick, the sorrowful, and the discontented, may find equal relief in solitude; it administers a balm to their tortured souls, heals the deep and painful wounds they have received, and in time restores them to their pristine health and vigor. The deceitful shrine in which the intoxication of sensuality involved health and happiness disappears, and they behold, in the place of imaginary joys, those objects only which afford real pleasure. Prosperity arrays every object in the most glowing and delightful colors; but to adversity every thing appears black and dismal. Nor are the errors of these contrary extremes discovered until the moment when the curtain drops, and dissipates the illusion: the deceitful dream continues until the imagination is silenced. The unhappy then perceive that the Almighty was watching over them, even when they conceived themselves entirely abandoned: the happy then discover the vanity of those pleasures and amusements to which they surrendered themselves so implicitly during the intoxication of the world, and reflect seriously upon their misconduct; upon their present state and future destiny; and upon the modes most likely to conduct them to true felicity. How miserable should we be, were the Divine Providence to grant us every thing we desire! At the very instant when we conceive all the happiness of our lives annihilated, God, perhaps, is performing something extraordinary in our favor. Certain it is, that patience and perseverance will, in solitude, convert the deepest sorrow into tranquillity and joy. Those objects which, at a distance, appear menacing, lose, on a nearer approach, their disagreeable aspect, and, in the event, frequently produce the most agreeable pleasures. He who tries every expedient, who boldly opposes himself to every difficulty, who steadily resists every obstacle, who neglects no exertion within his power, and relies with confidence on the assistance of God, extracts from affliction both its poison and its sting, and deprives misfortune of its victory.

Sorrow, misfortune, and sickness, soon render solitude easy and familiar to our minds. How willingly do we renounce the world, and become indifferent to all its pleasures, when the insidious eloquence of the passions is silenced, and our powers are debilitated by vexation or ill health! It is then we perceive the weakness of those succors which the world affords. How many useful truths, alas! has the bed of sickness and sorrow instilled even into the minds of kings and princes! truths which, in the hour of health, they would have been unable to learn amidst the deceitful counsels of their pretended friends. The time, indeed, in which a valetudinarian is capable of employing his powers with facility and success, in a manner conformable to his designs, is short, and runs rapidly away. Those only who enjoy robust health can exclaim, "Time is my own;" for he who labors under continual sickness and suffering, and whose avocations depend on the public necessity or caprice, can never say that he has one moment to himself. He must watch the fleeting hours as they pass, and seize an interval of leisure when and where he can. Necessity, as well as reason, convinces him that he must, in spite of his daily sufferings, his wearied body, or his harassed mind, firmly resist his accumulating troubles; and, if he would save himself from becoming the victim of dejection, he must manfully combat the difficulties by which he is attacked. The more we enervate ourselves, the more we become the prey of ill health; but determined courage, and obstinate resistance, frequently renovate our powers; and he who, in the calm of solitude, vigorously wrestles with misfortune, is, in the event, sure of gaining the victory.

The influence of the mind upon the body is a consolatory truth to those who are subject to constitutional complaints. Supported by this reflection, the efforts of reason continue unsubdued; the influence of religion maintains its empire; and the lamentable truth, that men of the finest sensibility, and most cultivated understanding, frequently possess less fortitude under affliction than the most vulgar of mankind, remains unknown. Campanella, incredible as it may seem, suffered by the indulgence of melancholy reflections, a species of mental torture more painful than any bodily torture could have produced. I can, however, from my own experience, assert, that, even in the extremity of distress, every object which diverts the attention, softens the evils we endure, and frequently drives them entirely away. By diverting the attention, many celebrated philosophers have been able not only to preserve a tranquil mind in the midst of the most poignant sufferings, but have even increased the strength of their intellectual faculties, in spite of their corporeal pains. Rousseau composed the greater part of his immortal works under the continual pressure of sickness and sorrow. Gellert, who, by his mild, agreeable, and instructive writings, has become the preceptor of Germany, certainly found, in this interesting occupation, the secret remedy against melancholy. Mendelsohm, at an age far advanced in life, and not, in general, subject to dejection, was for a long time oppressed by an almost inconceivable derangement of the nervous system; but, by submitting with patience and docility to his sufferings, he still maintains all the noble and high advantages of youth. Garve, who was for several years unable to read, to write, or even to think, has since produced his treatise upon Cicero, in which this profound writer, so circumspect in all his expressions that he appears hurt if any improper word escapes his pen, thanks the Almighty, with a sort of rapture, for the weakness of his constitution, because it had taught him the extraordinary influence which the powers of the mind have over those of the body.

Solitude is not merely desirable, but absolutely necessary, to those characters who possess sensibilities too quick, and imaginations too ardent, to live quietly in the world, and who are incessantly inveighing against men and things. Those who suffer their minds to be subdued by circumstances which would scarcely produce an emotion in other bosoms; who complain of the severity of their misfortunes on occasions which others would not feel; who are dispirited by every occurrence which does not produce immediate satisfaction and pleasure; who are incessantly tormented by the illusion of fancy; who are unhinged and dejected the moment prosperity is out of their view; who repine at what they possess, from an ignorance of what they really want; whose minds are for ever veering from one vain wish to another; who are alarmed at every thing, and enjoy nothing; are not formed for society, and, if solitude have no power to heal their wounded spirits, are certainly incurable.

Men who in other respects possess rational minds and pious dispositions, frequently fall into low spirits and despair; but it is in general almost entirely their own fault. If it proceed, as is generally the case, from unfounded fears; if they love to torment themselves and others on every trivial disappointment or slight indisposition; if they constantly resort to medicine for that relief which reason alone can bestow; if they fondly indulge, instead of repressing, these idle fancies; if, after having endured the most excruciating pains with patience, and supported the greatest misfortunes with fortitude, they neither can nor will learn to bear the puncture of the smallest pin, or those trifling adversities to which human life is unavoidably subject; they can only attribute their unhappy condition to their own misconduct; and, although they might, by no very irksome effort of their understandings, look with an eye of composure and tranquillity on the multiplied and fatal fires issuing from the dreadful cannon's mouth, will continue shamefully subdued by the idle apprehensions of being fired at by pop-guns.

All these qualities of the soul, fortitude, firmness, and stoic inflexibility, are much sooner acquired by silent meditation than amidst the noisy intercourse of mankind, where innumerable difficulties continually oppose us; where ceremony, servility, flattery, and fear, contaminate our dispositions; where every occurrence opposes our endeavors; and where, for this reason, men of the weakest minds, and the most contracted notions, become more active and popular, gain more attention, and are better received, than men of feeling hearts and liberal understandings.

The mind, in short, fortifies itself with impregnable strength in the bowers of solitary retirement against every species of suffering and affliction. The frivolous attachments which, in the world, divert the soul from its proper objects, and drive it wandering, as chance may direct, into an eccentric void, die away. Contented, from experience, with the little which nature requires, rejecting every superfluous desire, and having acquired a complete knowledge of ourselves, the visitations of the Almighty, when he chastises us with affliction, humbles our presumptuous pride, disappoints our vain conceits, restrains the violence of our passions, and makes us sensible of our inanity and weakness, are received with composure and felt without surprise. How many important truths do we here learn, of which the worldly minded man has no idea! Casting the eye of calm reflection on ourselves, and on the objects around us, how resigned we become to the lot of humanity! How different every object appears! The heart expands to every noble sentiment; the bloom of conscious virtue brightens on the cheek; the mind teems with sublime conceptions; and, boldly taking the right path, we at length reach the bowers of innocence, and the plains of peace.

On the death of a beloved friend, we constantly feel a strong desire to withdraw from society; but our worldly acquaintances unite in general to destroy this laudable inclination. Conceiving it improper to mention the subject of our grief, our companions, cold and indifferent to the event, surround us, and think their duties sufficiently discharged by paying the tributary visit, and amusing us with the current topics of the town. Such idle pleasantries cannot convey a balm of comfort into the wounded heart.

When I, alas! within two years after my arrival in Germany, lost the lovely idol of my heart, the amiable companion of my former days, I exclaimed a thousand times to my surrounding friends, *Oh! leave me to myself!* Her departed spirit still hovers round me: the tender recollection of her society, the afflicting remembrance of her sufferings on my account, are always present to my mind. What mildness and affability! Her death was as calm and resigned as her life was pure and virtuous. During five long months, the lingering pangs of dissolution hung continually around her. One day, as she reclined upon her pillow, while I read to her *"The Death of Christ,"* by Rammler, she cast her eyes over the page, and silently pointed out to me the following passage; "My breath grows weak, my days are shortened, my heart is full of affliction, and my soul prepares to take its flight." Alas! when I recall all those circumstances to my mind, and recollect how impossible it was for me to abandon the world at that moment of anguish and distress, when I carried the seeds of death within my bosom; when I had neither fortitude to bear my afflictions, nor courage to resist them, while I was yet pursued by malice, and traduced by calumny; I can easily conceive, in such a situation, that my exclamation might be, *leave me to myself.* To a heart thus torn by too rigorous a destiny from the bosom that was opened for its reception; from a bosom in which it fondly dwelt; from an object that it dearly loved, detached from every object, at a loss where to fix its affections or communicate its feelings, solitude alone can administer comfort.

Solitude, when it has ripened and preserved the tender and humane feelings of the heart, and created in the mind a salutary distrust of our vain reason and boasted abilities, may be considered to have brought us nearer to God. Humility is the first lesson we learn from reflection, and self distrust the first proof we give of having obtained a knowledge of ourselves. When, in attending the duties of my profession, I behold, on the bed of sickness, the efforts of the soul to oppose its impending dissolution, and discover, by the increasing torments of the patient, the rapid advances of death; when I see the unhappy sufferer extend his cold and trembling hands to thank the Almighty for the smallest mitigation of his pains; when I hear his utterance choked by intermingled groans, and view the tender looks, the silent anguish of his attending friends; all my fortitude abandons me; my heart bleeds; and I tear myself from the sorrowful scene, only to pour my tears more freely over the lamentable lot of humanity, to regret the inefficacy of those medical powers which I am supposed only to have sought with so much anxiety as a mean of prolonging my own miserable existence,

> "When in this vale of years I backward look,
>
> And miss such numbers, numbers too of such,
>
> Firmer in health, and greener in their age,
>
> And stricter on their guard, and fitter far
>
> To play life's subtle game, I scarce believe
>
> I still survive: and am I fond of life
>
> Who scarce can think it possible I live?
>
> Alive by miracle! If I am still alive,
>
> Who long have buried what gives life to live."

The wisdom that teaches us to avoid the snares of the world, is not to be acquired by the incessant pursuit of entertainments; by flying, without reflection, from one party to another; by continual conversation on low and trifling subjects; by undertaking every thing and doing nothing. "He who would acquire true wisdom," says a celebrated philosopher, "must learn to live in solitude." An uninterrupted course of dissipation stifles every virtuous sentiment. The dominion of reason is lost amidst the intoxications of pleasure; its voice is no longer heard; its authority is no longer obeyed; the mind no longer strives to surmount temptations; but instead of shunning the perils which the passions scatter in our way, we run eagerly to find them. The idea of God, and the precepts of his holy religion, are never so little remembered as in the ordinary intercourses of society. Engaged in a multiplicity of absurd pursuits, entranced in the delirium of gayety, inflamed by the continual ebriety which raises the passions and stimulates the desires, every connexion between God and man is dissolved; the bright and noble faculty of reason obscured; and even the great and important duties of religion, the only source of true felicity, totally obliterated from the mind, or remembered only with levity and indifference. On the contrary, he who, entering into a serious self-examination, elevates his thoughts in silence toward his God; who consults the theatre of nature, the spangled firmament of heaven, the meadows enamelled with flowers, the stupendous mountains, and the silent groves, as the temples of the Divinity; who directs the emotions of his heart to the great Author and Conductor of every thing; who has his enlightened providence continually before his eyes, must, most assuredly, have already lived in pious solitude and religious retirement.

The pious disposition which a zealous devotion to God engenders in solitude, may, it is true, in certain characters, and under particular circumstances, degenerate into the gloom of superstition, or rise into the phrenzy of fanaticism; but these excesses soon abate; and, compared with that fatal supineness which extinguishes every virtue, are really advantageous. The sophistry of the passions is silent during the serious hours of self-examination, and the perturbations we feel on the discovery of our errors and defects, is converted by the light of a pure and rational faith, into happy ease and perfect tranquillity. The fanatic enthusiast presents himself before the Almighty much oftener than the supercilious wit who derides an holy religion, and calls piety a weakness. Philosophy and morality become in solitude the handmaids of religion, and join their powers to conduct us into the bowers of eternal peace. They teach us to examine our hearts, and exhort us to guard against the dangers of fanaticism. But if virtue cannot be instilled into the soul without convulsive efforts, they also admonish us not to be intimidated by the apprehension of danger. It is not in the moment of joy, when we turn our eyes from God and our thoughts from eternity, that we experience those salutary fervors of the soul, which even religion, with all her powers, cannot produce so soon as a mental affliction or a corporeal malady. The celebrated M. Grave, one of the greatest philosophers of Germany, exclaimed to Dr. Spalding and myself, "I am indebted to my malady for having led me to make a closer scrutiny and more accurate observation on my own character."

In the last moments of life, it is certain that we all wish we had passed our days in greater privacy and solitude, in stricter intimacy with ourselves, and in closer communion with God. Pressed by the recollection of our errors, we then clearly perceive that they were occasioned by not having shunned the snares of the world, and by not having watched with sufficient care over the inclinations of our hearts. Oppose the sentiments of a solitary man, who has passed his life in pious conference with God, to those which occupy a worldly mind, forgetful of its Creator, and sacrificing its dearest interests to the enjoyment of the moment: compare the character of a wise man, who reflects in silence on the importance of eternity, with that of a fashionable being, who consumes all his time at ridottos, balls, and assemblies; and we shall then perceive that solitude, dignified retirement, select friendships, and rational society, can alone afford true pleasure, and give us what all the vain enjoyments of the world will never bestow, consolation in death, and hope of everlasting life. But the bed of death discovers most clearly the difference between the just man, who has quietly passed his days in religious contemplation, and the man of the world, whose thoughts have only been employed to feed his passions and gratify his desires. A life passed amidst the tumultuous dissipations of the world, even when unsullied by the commission of any positive crime, concludes, alas! very differently from that which has been spent in the bowers of solitude, adorned by innocence, and rewarded by virtue.

But, as example teaches more effectually than precept, and curiosity is more alive to recent facts than remote illustrations, I shall here relate the history of a man of family and fashion, who a few years since shot himself in London; from which it will appear, that men possessed even of the best feelings of the heart, may be rendered extremely miserable, by suffering their principles to be corrupted by the practice of the world.

The honorable Mr. Damer, the eldest son of Lord Milton, was five and thirty years of age when he put a period to his existence by means perfectly correspondent to the principles in which he had lived. He was married to a rich lady, the daughter-in-law of General Conway. Nature had endowed him with extraordinary talents; but a most infatuated fondness for excessive dissipation obscured the brightest faculties of his mind, and perverted many of the excellent qualities of the heart. His houses, his carriages, his horses, and his liveries, surpassed in splendor and magnificence every thing sumptuous and costly even in the superb and extravagant metropolis of Great Britain. The fortune he possessed was great; but the variety of lavish expenditures in which he engaged exceeded his income, and he was reduced at length to the necessity of borrowing money. He raised, in different ways, near forty thousand pounds, the greater part of which he employed with improvident generosity in relieving the distresses of his less opulent companions; for his heart overflowed with tenderness and compassion; but this exquisite sensibility, which was ever alive to the misfortunes of others, was at length awakened to his own embarrassed situation; and his mind driven by the seeming irretrievable condition of his affairs, to the utmost verge of despair. Retiring to a common brothel, he sent for four women of the town, and passed several hours in their company with apparent good spirits and unencumbered gayety; but, when the dead of night arrived, he requested of them, with visible dejection, to retire; and immediately afterward drawing from his pocket a pistol, which he had carried about him the whole afternoon, blew out his brains. It appeared that he had passed the evening with these women in the same manner as he had been used to pass many others with different women of the same description, without demanding favours which they would most willingly have granted, and only desiring, in return for the money he lavished on them, the dissipation of their discourse, or at most, the ceremony of a salute, to divert the sorrow that preyed upon his tortured mind. But the gratitude he felt for the temporary oblivion which these intercourses afforded, sometimes ripened into feelings of the warmest friendship. A celebrated actress of the London theatre, whose conversations had already drained him of considerable sums of money, requested of him, only three days before his death, to send her five and twenty guineas. At that moment he had only ten guineas about him; but he sent her, with an apology for his inability to comply immediately with her request, all he had, and soon afterward borrowed the remainder of the money, and sent it to her without delay. This unhappy young man, shortly before the fatal catastrophe, had written to his father, and disclosed to him the distressed situation he was in; and the very night on which he terminated his existence, his affectionate parent, the good Lord Milton, arrived in London, for the purpose of discharging all the debts, and arranging the affairs of his unhappy son. Thus lived and died this destitute and dissipated man! How different from that life which the innocent live, or that death which the virtuous die!

I hope I may be permitted in this place to relate the story of a young lady whose memory I am extremely anxious to preserve; for I can with great truth say of her, as Petrarch said of his beloved Laura, "the world was unacquainted with the excellence of her character: for she was only known to those whom she has left behind to bewail her loss." Solitude was all the world she knew; for her only pleasures were those which a retired and virtuous life affords. Submitting with pious resignation to the dispensations of heaven, her weak frame sustained, with steady fortitude, every affliction of mortality. Mild, good, and tender, she endured her sufferings without a murmur or sigh; and although naturally timid and reserved, disclosed the feelings of her soul with all the warmth of filial enthusiasm. Of this description was the superior character of whom I now write; a character who convinced me, by her fortitude under the severest misfortunes, how much strength solitude is capable of conveying to the mind even of the feeblest being. Diffident of her own powers, she listened to the precepts of a fond parent, and relied with perfect confidence on the goodness of God. Taught by my experience, submitting to my judgment, she entertained for me the most ardent affection; and convinced me, not by professions, but by actions, of her sincerity. Willingly would I have sacrificed my life to have saved her; and I am satisfied that she would as willingly have given up her own for me. I had no pleasure but in pleasing her, and my endeavors for that purpose were most gratefully returned. A rose was my favorite flower, and she presented one to me almost daily during the season. I received it from her hand with the highest delight, and cherished it as the richest treasure. A malady of almost a singular kind, a hæmorrhage in the lungs, suddenly deprived me of the comfort of this beloved child, and tore her from my protecting arms. From the knowledge I had of her constitution, I immediately perceived that the disorder was mortal. How frequently during that fatal day did my wounded, bleeding heart, bend me on my knees before God to supplicate for her recovery. But I concealed my feelings from her observation. Although sensible of her danger, she never discovered the least apprehension of its approach. Smiles played around her pallid cheeks whenever I entered or quitted the room; and when worn down by the fatal distemper, a prey to the most corroding grief, a victim to the sharpest and most intolerable pains, she made no complaint; but mildly answered all my questions by some short sentence, without entering into any detail. Her decay and impending dissolution became obvious to the eye; but to the last moment of her life, her countenance preserved a serenity correspondent to the purity of her mind, and the affectionate tenderness of her heart. Thus I beheld my dear and only daughter, at the age of five and twenty, after a lingering suffering of nine long, long months, expire in my arms. So long and so severe an attack was not necessary to the conquest: she had been the submissive victim of ill health from her earliest infancy; her appetite was almost gone when we left Swisserland: a residence which she quitted with her usual sweetness of temper, and without discovering the smallest regret: although a young man, as handsome in his person as he was amiable in the qualities of his mind, the object of her first, her only affection, a few weeks afterward put a period to his existence. During the few happy days we passed at Hanover, where she rendered herself universally respected and beloved, she amused herself by composing religious prayers, which were afterward found among her papers, and in which she implores death to afford her a speedy relief from her pains. During the same period she wrote also many letters, always affecting, and frequently sublime. They were couched in expressions of the same desire speedily to reunite her soul with the Author of her days. The last words that my dear, my beloved child uttered, amidst the most painful agonies, were these—"To-day I shall taste the joys of heaven!"

How unworthy of this bright example should we be, if, after having seen the severest sufferings sustained by a female in the earliest period of life, and of the weakest constitution, we permitted our minds to be dejected by misfortunes which courage might enable us to surmount! A female who under the anguish of inexpressible torments, never permitted a sigh or complaint to escape from her lips, but submitted with silent resignation to the will of heaven, in hope of meeting with reward hereafter. She was ever active, invariably mild, and always compassionate to the miseries of others. But we, who have before our eyes the sublime instructions which a character thus virtuous and noble has here given us; we, who like her, aspire to a seat in the mansions of the blessed, refuse the smallest sacrifice, make no endeavor to stem with courage the torrent of adversity, or to acquire that degree of patience and resignation, which a strict examination of our own hearts, and silent communion with God, would certainly afford.

Sensible and unfortunate beings! The slight misfortunes by which you are now oppressed, and driven to despair (for slight, indeed, they are, when compared with mine,) will ultimately raise your minds above the low considerations of the world, and give a strength to your power which you now conceive to be impossible. You now think yourselves sunk into the deepest abyss of suffering and sorrow; but the time will soon arrive when you will perceive yourselves in that happy state in which the mind verges from earth and fixes its attention on heaven. You will then enjoy a calm repose, be susceptible of pleasures equally substantial and sublime, and possess in lieu of tumultuous anxieties for life, the serene and comfortable hope of immortality. Blessed, supremely blessed, is he who knows the value of retirement and tranquillity, who is capable of enjoying the silence of the groves, and all the pleasures of rural solitude. The soul then tastes celestial delight even under the deepest impressions of sorrow and dejection; regains its strength, collects new courage, and acts with perfect freedom. The eye then looks with fortitude on the transient sufferings of disease; the mind no longer feels the dread of being alone; and we learn to cultivate, during the remainder of our lives, a bed of roses round even the tomb of death.

Chapter V
Advantages of solitude in exile

The advantages of solitude are not confined to rank, or fortune, or to circumstances. Fragrant breezes, magnificent forests, richly tinted meadows, and that endless variety of beautiful objects which the birth of spring spreads over the face of nature, enchant not only philosophers, kings, and heroes, but ravish the mind of the meanest spectator with exquisite delight. An English author has very justly observed, that "it is not necessary that he who looks with pleasure on the color of a flower, should study the principles of vegetation; or that the Ptolemaic and Copernican systems should be compared, before the light of the sun can gladden, or its warmth invigorate. Novelty in itself is a source of gratification; and Milton justly observes, that to him who has been long pent up in cities, no rural object can be presented which will not delight or refresh some of his senses."

Exiles themselves frequently experience the advantages and enjoyments of solitude. Instead of the world from which they are banished, they form, in the tranquillity of retirement, a new world for themselves; forget the false joys and fictitious pleasures which they followed in the zenith of greatness, habituate their minds to others of a nobler kind, more worthy the attention of rational beings; and to pass their days with tranquillity, invent a variety of innocent felicities, which are only thought of at a distance from society, far removed from all consolation, far from their country, their families, and their friends.

But exiles, if they wish to insure happiness in retirement, must, like other men, fix their minds upon some one object, and adopt the pursuit of it in such a way as to revive their buried hopes, or to excite the prospect of approaching pleasure.

Maurice, prince of Isenbourg, distinguished himself by his courage during a service of twenty years under Ferdinand, duke of Brunswick, and Marshal Broglio, and in the war between the Russians and the Turks. Health and repose were sacrificed to the gratification of his ambition and love of glory. During his service in the Russian army, he fell under the displeasure of the empress, and was sent into exile. The calamitous condition to which persons exiled by this government are reduced is well known; but this philosophic prince contrived to render even a Russian banishment agreeable. While oppressed both in body and mind by the painful reflections which his situation at first created, and reduced by his anxieties to a mere skeleton, he accidentally met with the little essay written by Lord Bolingbroke on the subject of Exile. He read it several times, and, "in proportion to the number of times I read," said the prince, in the preface to the elegant and nervous translation he made of this work, "I felt all my sorrows and disquietudes vanish."

This essay by Lord Bolingbroke upon exile, is a master-piece of stoic philosophy and fine writing. He there boldly examines all the adversities of life. "Let us," says he, "set all our past and present afflictions at once before our eyes: let us resolve to overcome them instead of flying from them, or wearing out the sense of them with long and ignominious patience. Instead of palliating remedies, let us use the incision knife and the caustic, search the wound to the bottom, and work an immediate and radical cure."

Perpetual banishment, like uninterrupted solitude, certainly strengthens the powers of the mind, and enables the sufferer to collect sufficient force to support his misfortunes. Solitude, indeed, becomes an easy situation to those exiles who are inclined to indulge the pleasing sympathies of the heart; for they then experience pleasures that were before unknown, and from that moment forget those they tasted in the more flourishing and prosperous conditions of life.

Brutus, when he visited the banished Marcellus in his retreat at Mitylene, found him enjoying the highest felicities of which human nature is susceptible, and devoting his time, as before his banishment, to the study of every useful science. Deeply impressed by the example this unexpected scene afforded, he felt, on his return, that it was Brutus who was exiled, and not Marcellus whom he left behind. Quintus Metellus Numidicus had experienced the like fate a few years before. While the Roman people, under the guidance of Marius were laying the foundation of that tyranny which Cesar afterward completed, Metellus, singly, in the midst of an alarmed senate, and surrounded by an enraged populace, refused to take the oath imposed by the pernicious laws of the tribune Saturnius; and his intrepid conduct was converted, by the voice of faction, into a high crime against the state; for which he was dragged from his senatorial seat by the licentious rabble, exposed to the indignity of a public impeachment, and sentenced to perpetual exile. The more virtuous citizens, however, took arms in his defence, and generously resolved rather to perish than behold their country unjustly deprived of so much merit: but this magnanimous Roman, whom no persuasion could induce to do wrong, declined to increase the confusion of the commonwealth by encouraging resistance, conceiving it a duty he owed to the laws, not to suffer any sedition to take place on his account. Contenting himself with protesting his innocence, and sincerely lamenting the public phrenzy, he exclaimed, as Plato had done before during the distractions of the Athenian commonwealth, "If the times should mend, I shall recover my station; if not, it is a happiness to be absent from Rome;" and departed without regret into exile, fully convinced of its advantages to a mind incapable of finding repose except on foreign shores, and which at Rome must have been incessantly tortured by the hourly sight of a sickly state and an expiring republic.

Rutilius also, feeling the same contempt for the sentiments and manners of the age, voluntarily withdrew himself from the corrupted metropolis of the republic. Asia had been defended by his integrity and courage against the ruinous and oppressive extortion of the publicans. These noble and spirited exertions, which he was prompted to make not only from his high sense of justice, but in the honourable discharge of the particular duties of his office, drew on him the indignation of the equestrian order, and excited the animosity of the faction which supported the interests of Marius. They induced the vile and infamous Apicius to become the instrument of his destruction. He was accused of corruption; and as the authors and abettors of this false accusation sat as judges on his trial, Rutilius, the most innocent and virtuous citizen of the republic, was of course condemned: for, indeed, he scarcely condescended to defend the cause. Seeking an asylum in the east, this truly respectable Roman, whose merits were not only overlooked, but traduced, by his ungrateful country, was every where received with profound veneration and unqualified applause. He had however, before the term of his exile expired, an opportunity of exhibiting the just contempt he felt for the treatment he had received; for when Sylla earnestly solicited him to return to Rome, he not only refused to comply with his request, but removed his residence to a greater distance from his infatuated country.

Cicero, however, who possessed in an eminent degree all the resources and sentiments which are necessary to render solitude pleasant and advantageous, is a memorable exception to these instances of happy and contented exiles. This eloquent patriot, who had been publicly proclaimed, "the saviour of his country," who had pursued his measures with undaunted perseverance, in defiance of the open menaces of a desperate faction, and the concealed daggers of hired assassins, sunk into dejection and dismay under a sentence of exile. The strength of his constitution had long been impaired by incessant anxiety and fatigue; and the terrors of banishment so oppressed his mind, that he lost all his powers, and became, from the deep melancholy into which it plunged him, totally incapable of adopting just sentiments, or pursuing spirited measures. By this weak and unmanly conduct he disgraced an event by which Providence intended to render his glory complete. Undetermined where to go, or what to do, he lamented, with effeminate sighs and childish tears, that he could now no longer enjoy the luxuries of his fortune, the splendor of his rank, or the charms of his popularity. Weeping over the ruins of his magnificent mansion, which Clodius levelled with the ground, and groaning for the absence of his wife, Terentia, whom he soon afterward repudiated, he suffered the deepest melancholy to seize upon his mind: became a prey to the most inveterate grief; complained with bitter anguish of wants, which, if supplied, would have afforded him no enjoyment; and acted, in short, so ridiculously, that both his friends and his enemies concluded that adversity had deranged his mind. Cesar beheld with secret and malignant pleasure, the man who had refused to act as his lieutenant, suffering under the scourge of Clodius. Pompey hoped that all sense of *his* ingratitude would be effaced by the contempt and derision to which a benefactor, whom he had shamefully abandoned, thus meanly exposed his character. Atticus himself, whose mind was bent on magnificence and money, and who, by his temporizing talents, endeavored to preserve the friendship of all parties, without enlisting in any, blushed for the unmanly conduct of Cicero; and in the censorial style of Cato, instead of his own plausible dialect, severely reproached him for continuing so meanly attached to his former fortunes. Solitude had no influence over a mind so weak and depressed as to turn the worst side of every subject to its view. He died, however, with greater heroism than he lived; "approach, old soldier!" cried he, from his litter, to Popilius Lœnas, his former client and present murderer, "and, if you have the courage, take my life."

"These instances," says Lord Bolingbroke, "show that as change of place, simply considered, can render no man unhappy; so the other evils which are objected to exile, either cannot happen to wise and virtuous men, or, if they do happen to them, cannot render them miserable. Stones are hard, and cakes of ice are cold, and all who feel them feel alike; but the good or the bad events which fortune brings upon us, are felt according to the qualities that we, not they, possess. They are in themselves indifferent and common accidents, and they acquire strength by nothing but our vice or our weakness. Fortune can dispense neither felicity nor infelicity, unless we co-operate with her. Few men who are unhappy under the loss of an estate, would be happy in the possession of it; and those who deserve to enjoy the advantages which exile takes away, will not be unhappy when they are deprived of them."

An exile, however, cannot hope to see his days glide quietly away in rural delights and philosophic repose, except he has conscientiously discharged those duties which he owed to the world, and given that example of rectitude to future ages which every character exhibits who is as great after his fall as he was at the most brilliant period of his prosperity.

Chapter VI
Advantages of solitude in old age; and on the bed of death

The decline of life, and particularly the condition of old age, derive from solitude the purest sources of uninterrupted enjoyment. Old age when considered as a period of comparative quietude and repose, as a serious and contemplative interval between a transitory existence and an approaching immortality, is, perhaps, the most agreeable condition of human life: a condition to which solitude affords a secure harbor against those shattering tempests to which the frail bark of man is continually exposed in the short but dangerous voyage of the world; a harbor from whence he may securely view the rocks and quicksands which threatened his destruction, and which he has happily escaped.

Men are by nature disposed to investigate the various properties of distant objects before they think of contemplating their own characters; like modern travellers who visit foreign countries before they are acquainted with their own. But prudence will exhort the young, and experience teach the aged, to conduct themselves on very different principles; and both the one and the other will find that solitude and self-examination are the beginning and the end of true wisdom.

> Oh! lost to virtue, lost to manly thought,
>
> Lost to the noble sallies of the soul!
>
> Who think in solitude to be alone.
>
> Communion sweet; communion large and high.
>
> Our reason, guardian angel, and our God:
>
> The nearest these when others most remote;
>
> And all, ere long, shall be remote but these.

The levity of youth, by this communion large and high, will be repressed, and the depression which sometimes accompanies old age entirely removed. An unceasing succession of gay hopes, fond desires, ardent wishes, high delights, and unfounded fancies, form the character of our early years; but those which follow are marked with melancholy and increasing sorrows. A mind, however that is invigorated by observation and experience, remains dauntless and unmoved, amidst both the prosperities and adversities of life. He who is no longer forced to exert his powers, and who at an early period of his life has well studied the manners of men, will complain very little of the ingratitude with which his favors and anxieties have been requited. All he asks is, that the world will let him alone: and having a thorough knowledge not only of his own character, but of mankind, he is enabled to enjoy the comforts of repose.

It is finely remarked by a celebrated German, that there are political as well as religious Carthusians, and that both orders are sometimes composed of most excellent and pious characters. "It is," says this admirable writer, "in the deepest and most sequestered recesses of forests that we meet with the peaceful sage, the calm observer, the friend of truth, and the lover of his country, who renders himself beloved by his wisdom, revered for his knowledge, respected for his veracity, and adored for his benevolence; whose confidence and friendship every one is anxious to gain; and who excites admiration by the eloquence of his conversation, and esteem by the virtue of his actions, while he raises wonder by the obscurity of his name, and the mode of his existence. The giddy multitude solicit him to relinquish his solitude, and seat himself on the throne: but they perceive inscribed on his forehead, beaming with sacred fire, *odi profanum vulgus et arceo*; and instead of being his seducers, become his disciples." But, alas! this extraordinary character, whom I saw some years ago in Weteravia, who inspired me with filial reverence and affection, and whose animated countenance announced the superior wisdom and happy tranquillity of his mind, is now no more. There did not perhaps at that time exist in any court a more profound statesman: he was intimately acquainted with all, and corresponded personally with some of the most celebrated sovereigns of Europe. I never met with an observer who penetrated with such quick and accurate sagacity into the minds and characters of men, who formed such true opinions of the world, or criticised with such discerning accuracy the actions of those who were playing important parts on its various theatres. There never was a mind more free, more enlarged, more powerful, or more engaging; or an eye more lively and inquisitive. He was the man, of all others, in whose company I could have lived with the highest pleasure, and died with the greatest comfort. The rural habitation in which he lived, was simple in its structure, and modest in its attire; the surrounding grounds and gardens laid out in the happy simplicity of nature; and his fare healthy and frugal. I never felt a charm more powerful than that which filled my bosom while I contemplated the happy solitude of the venerable Baron de Schautenbach at Weteravia.

Rousseau, feeling his end approach, also passed the few remaining years of an uneasy life in solitude. It was during old age that he composed the best and greater part of his admirable works; but, although he employed his time with judicious activity, his feelings had been too deeply wounded by the persecutions of the world, to enable him to find complete tranquillity in the bowers of retirement. Unhappily he continued ignorant of the danger of his situation, until the vexations of his mind, the disorders of his body, and his unpardonable neglect of health, had rendered his recovery impossible. It was not until he had been many years tormented by physicians, and racked by a painful malady, that he took up his pen; and his years increased only to increase the visible effect of his mental and corporeal afflictions, which at length became so acute, that he frequently raved wildly or fainted away under the excess of his pains.

It is observed by one of our refined critics, that "all Rousseau wrote during his old age is the effect of madness." "Yes," replied his fair friend, with greater truth, "but he raved so pleasantly, that we are delighted to run mad with him."

The mind becomes more disposed to seek its "guardian angel and its God," the nearer it approaches the confines of mortality. When the ardent fire of youth is extinguished, and the meridian heat of life's short day subsides into the soft tranquillity and refreshing quietude of its evening, we feel the important necessity of devoting some few hours to pious meditation before we close our eyes in endless night; and the very idea of being able to possess this interval of holy leisure, and to hold this sacred communion with God, recreates the mind, like the approach of spring after a dull, a dreary, and a distressing winter.

Petrarch scarcely perceived the approaches of old age. By constant activity he contrived to render retirement always happy, and year after year rolled unperceived away in pleasures and tranquillity. Seated in a verdant arbor in the vicinity of a Carthusian monastery, about three miles from Milan, he wrote to his friend Settimo with a simplicity of heart unknown in modern times. "Like a wearied traveller, I increase my pace in proportion as I approach the end of my journey, I pass my days and nights in reading and writing; these agreeable occupations alternately relieve each other, and are the only sources from whence I derive my pleasures. I lie awake and think, and divert my mind by every means in my power; and my ardor increases as new difficulties arise. Novelties incite, and obstacles sharpen, my resistance. The labors I endure are certain, for my hand is tired of holding my pen: but whether I shall reap the harvest of my toils I cannot tell. I am anxious to transmit my name to posterity: but if I am disappointed in this wish I am satisfied the age in which I live, or at least my friends, will know me, and this fame will satisfy me. My health is so good, my constitution so robust, and my temperament so warm, that neither the advance of years nor the most serious occupation, have power to conquer the rebellious enemy by which I am incessantly attacked. I should certainly become its victim, as I have frequently been, if Providence did not protect me. On the approach of spring, I take up arms against the flesh, and am even at this moment struggling for my liberty against this dangerous enemy."

A rural retreat, however lonely or obscure, contributes to increase the fame of those great and noble characters who relinquish the world at an advanced period of their lives, and pass the remainder of their days in solitude: their lustre beams from their retirement with brighter rays than those which shone around them in their earliest days, and on the theatre of their glory. "It is in solitude, in exile, and on the bed of death," says Pope, "that the noblest characters of antiquity shone with the greatest splendor; it was then they performed the greatest services; for it was during those periods that they became useful examples." And Rousseau appears to have entertained the same opinion: "It is noble," says he, "to exhibit to the eyes of men an example of the life they ought to lead. The man who, when age or ill health has deprived him of activity, dares to resound from his retreat the voice of truth, and to announce to mankind the folly of those opinions which render them miserable, is a public benefactor. I should be of much less use to my countrymen, were I to live among them, than I can possibly be in my retreat. Of what importance can it be, whether I live in one place or in another, provided I discharge my duties properly?"

A certain young lady of Germany, however, was of opinion that Rousseau was not entitled to praise. She maintained that he was a dangerous corrupter of the youthful mind, and that he had very improperly discharged his duties, by discovering in his Confessions the moral defects and vicious inclinations of his heart. "Such a work written by a man of virtue," said she, "would render him an object of abhorrence: but Rousseau, whose writings are circulated to captivate the wicked, proves, by his story of the Ruban Vole, that he possesses a heart of the blackest dye. It is evident, from many passages in that publication, that it was vanity alone which guided his pen; and from many others, that he felt himself conscious he was disclosing falsehoods. There is nothing, in short, throughout the work that bears the stamp of truth; and all it informs us of is, that Madame de Warens was the original from which he drew the character of Julia. These unjustly celebrated Confessions contain, generally speaking, a great many fine words, and but very few good thoughts. If, instead of rejecting every opportunity of advancing himself in life, he had engaged in some industrious profession, he might have been more useful to the world than he has been by the publication of his dangerous writings."

This incomparable criticism upon Rousseau merits preservation; for, in my opinion, it is the only one of its kind. The Confessions of Rousseau is a work certainly not proper for the eye of youth; but to me it appears one of the most remarkable philosophic publications that the present age has produced. The fine style and enchanting colors in which it is written are its least merits. The most distant posterity will read it with rapture, without inquiring what age the venerable author had attained when he gave to the world this last proof of his sincerity.

Age, however advanced, is capable of enjoying real pleasure. A virtuous old man passes his days with serene gayety, and receives, in the happiness he feels from the benedictions of all around him, a rich reward for the rectitude and integrity of his past life; for the mind reviews with joyful satisfaction its honorable and self-approving transactions: nor does the near prospect of the tomb give fearful emotion to his undismayed and steady soul.

The empress Maria Theresa has caused her own mausoleum to be erected, and frequently, accompanied by her family, visits with serenity and composure, a monumental depository, the idea of which conveys such painful apprehension to almost every mind. Pointing it out to the observation of her children, "Ought we to be proud or arrogant," says she, "when we here behold the tomb in which, after a few years, the poor remains of royalty must quietly repose?"

There are few men capable of thinking with so much sublimity. Every one, however, is capable of retiring, at least occasionally, from the corruptions of the world; and if, during this calm retreat, they shall happily learn to estimate their past days with propriety, and to live the remainder in private virtue and public utility, the tomb will lose its menacing aspect, and death appear like the calm evening of a fine and well spent day.

> "Blest be that hand divine, which gently laid
>
> My heart at rest beneath this humble shed.
>
> The world's a stately bark on dang'rous seas,
>
> With pleasure seen, but boarded at our peril;
>
> Here, on a single plank, thrown safe ashore,
>
> I hear the tumult of the distant throng,

As that of seas remote, or dying storms;

And meditate on scenes more silent still;

Pursue my theme, and fight the fear of death.

Here, like a shepherd gazing from his hut,

Touching his reed, or leaning on his staff,

Eager ambition's fiery chase I see;

I see the circling hunt of noisy men

Burst law's enclosure, leap the mounds of right,

Pursuing and pursued, each other's prey,

As wolves for rapine; as the fox for wiles;

Till death, that mighty hunter, earths them all."

When Addison perceived that he was given over by his physicians, and felt his end approaching, he sent for Lord Warwick, a young man of very irregular life and loose opinions, whom he had diligently, but vainly endeavored to reclaim, but who by no means wanted respect for the person of his preceptor, and was sensible of the loss he was about to sustain. When he entered the chamber of his dying friend, Addison, who was extremely feeble, and whose life at that moment hung quivering on his lips, observed a profound silence. The youth, after a long and awful pause, at length said, in low and trembling accents, "Sir, you desired to see me: signify your commands, and be assured I will execute them with religious fidelity." Addison took him by the hand, and with his expiring breath replied, "observe with what tranquillity a Christian can die." Such is the consolation which springs from a due sense of the principles, and a proper practice of the precepts of our holy religion: such is the high reward a life of simplicity and innocence bestows.

He who during the retirement of the day seriously studies, and during the silence of the night piously contemplates the august doctrines of revelation, will be convinced of their power by experiencing their effect. He will review with composure his past errors in society, perceive with satisfaction his present comfort in solitude, and aspire with hope to future happiness in heaven. He will think with the freedom of a philosopher, live with the piety of a Christian, and renounce with ease the poisonous pleasures of society from a conviction that they weaken the energies of his mind, and prevent his heart from raising itself toward his God. Disgusted with the vanities and follies of public life, he will retire into privacy, and contemplate the importance of eternity. Even if he be still obliged occasionally to venture on the stormy sea of busy life, he will avoid with greater skill and prudence the rocks and sands by which he is surrounded, and steer with greater certainty and effect from the tempests which most threaten his destruction; rejoicing less at the pleasant course which a favorable wind and clear sky may afford him, than at his having happily eluded such a multitude of dangers.

The hours consecrated to God in solitude, are not only the most important, but when we are habituated to this holy communion, the happiest of our lives. Every time we silently elevate our thoughts toward the great Author of our being, we recur to a contemplation of ourselves: and being rendered sensible of our nearer approach, not only in idea, but in reality, to the seat of eternal felicity, we retire, without regret, from the noisy multitude of the world. A philosophic view and complete knowledge of the nature of the species creep by degrees upon the mind: we scrutinize our characters with greater severity; feel with redoubled force the necessity of a reformation; and reflect with substantial effect on the glorious end for which we were created. Conscious that human actions are acceptable to the Almighty mind only in proportion as they are prompted by motives of the purest virtue, men ought benevolently to suppose that every good work springs from an untainted source and is performed merely for the benefit of mankind; but human actions are exposed to the influence of a variety of secondary causes, and cannot always be the pure production of an unbiassed heart. Good works, however, from whatever motive they arise, always convey a certain satisfaction and complacency to the mind. But when the real merit of the performer is to be actually investigated, the inquiry must always be, whether the mind was not actuated by sinister views, by the hope of gratifying a momentary passion, by the feelings of self love, rather than by the sympathies of brotherly affection: and these subtle and important questions are certainly discussed with closer scrutiny, and the motives of the heart explored and developed with greater sincerity, during those hours when we are alone before God than in any other situation.

Firm and untainted virtue, indeed, cannot be so easily and efficaciously acquired, as by practising the precepts of Christianity in the bowers of solitude. Religion refines our moral sentiments, disengages the heart from every vain desire, renders it tranquil under misfortunes, humble in the presence of God, and steady in the society of men. A life passed in the practice of every virtue, affords us a rich reward for all the hours we have consecrated to its duties, and enables us in the silence of solitude to raise our pure hands and chaste hearts in pious adoration to our Almighty Father!

How "low, flat, stale, and unprofitable, seem all the uses of this world," when the mind, boldly soaring beyond this lower sphere, indulges the idea that the pleasures which result from a life of innocence and virtue may be faintly analogous to the felicities of heaven! At least, I trust we may be permitted unoffendingly to conceive, according to our worldly apprehensions, that a free and unbounded liberty of thought and action, a high admiration of the universal system of nature, a participation of the divine essence, a perfect communion of friendship, and a pure interchange of love, may be a portion of the enjoyments we hope to experience in those regions of peace and happiness where no impure or improper sentiment can taint the mind. But notions like these, although they agreeably flatter our imaginations, shed at present but a glimmering light upon this awful subject, and must continue, like dreams and visions of the mind, until the clouds and thick darkness which surrounded the tomb of mortality no longer obscure the bright glories of everlasting life; until the veil shall be rent asunder, and the Eternal shall reveal those things which no eye hath seen, no ear has heard, and, which passeth all understanding. For I acknowledge, with awful reverence and silent submission, that the knowledge of eternity is to the human intellect like that which the color of crimson appeared to be in the mind of a blind man, who compared it to the sound of a trumpet. I cannot, however, conceive, that a notion more comfortable can be entertained, than that eternity promises a constant and uninterrupted tranquillity; although I am perfectly conscious that it is impossible to form an adequate idea of the nature of that enjoyment which is produced by happiness without end. An everlasting tranquillity is, in my imagination, the highest possible felicity, because I know of no felicity upon earth higher than that which a peaceful mind and contented heart afford.

Since, therefore, internal and external tranquillity is, upon earth, an incontestable commencement of beatitude, it may be extremely useful to believe, that a rational and qualified seclusion from the tumults of the world, may so highly rectify the faculties of the human soul, as to enable us to acquire in "blissful solitude" the elements of that happiness we expect to enjoy in the world to come.

> He is the happy man, whose life e'en now,
>
> Shows somewhat of that happier life to come:
>
> Who, doom'd to an obscure but tranquil state,
>
> Is pleas'd with it, and, were he free to choose
>
> Would make his fate his choice: whom peace, the fruit
>
> Of virtue, and whom virtue, fruit of faith,
>
> Prepare for happiness; bespeak him one
>
> Content, indeed, to sojourn while he must
>
> Below the skies, but having there his home,
>
> The world o'erlooks him in her busy search

Of objects more illustrious in her view;
And occupied as earnestly as she;
Though more sublimely, he o'erlooks the world.
She scorns his pleasures, for she knows them not;
He seeks not hers, for he has proved them vain.
He cannot skim the ground like such rare birds
Pursuing gilded flies, and such he deems
Her honors, her emoluments, her joys.
Therefore in contemplation is his bliss,
Whose power is such, that whom she lifts from earth
She makes familiar with a heaven unseen,
And shows him glories yet to be reveal'd.

FOOTNOTES

[1] Dissertatio Physiologica de irritabilitate quam publice defendet. Joh. Georgius Zimmerman. Goett. 4to. 1751.

[2] The following is a correct list of his writings, in the order in which they appear to have been published:

1. Dissertatio Inauguralis de Irritabilitate, 4to. Gottingen, 1751.

2. The life of Professor Haller, 8vo. Zurich, 1755.

3. Thoughts on the earthquake which was felt on the 9th of December, 1755, in Swisserland, 4to. 1756.

4. The Subversion of Lisbon, a Poem, 4to. 1776.

5. Meditations on Solitude, 8vo. 1756.

6. Essay on National Pride, 8vo. Zurich, 1764.

7. Treatise on Experience in Physic, 8vo. Zurich, 1764.

8. Treatise on the Dysentery, 8vo. Zurich, 1767.

9. Essay on Solitude, 4to. 1773.

10. Essay on Lavator's Phisiognomy. Hanover, 1778.

11. Essays, consisting of agreeable and instructive Tales, 8vo. 1779.

12. Conversations with the king of Prussia.

13. Treatise on Frederick the Great, 1788.

14. Select views of the Life, Reign and Character of Frederick the Great.

15. A variety of works published in the Helvetic Journal and in the Journals of the Physiological Society at Zurich.

16. A Work on Zoology.

[3] The king only survived the departure of his physician five weeks; he died on the 11th of August, 1786.

[4] Hœnigsberg.